Ultimate Academic Writing Hacks

Ultimate Academic Writing Hacks

Simple strategies for better essays, reports and dissertations

Ryan Arthur

BLOOMSBURY ACADEMIC
LONDON • NEW YORK • OXFORD • NEW DELHI • SYDNEY

BLOOMSBURY ACADEMIC

Bloomsbury Publishing Plc, 50 Bedford Square, London, WC1B 3DP, UK
Bloomsbury Publishing Inc, 1359 Broadway, New York, NY 10018, USA
Bloomsbury Publishing Ireland, 29 Earlsfort Terrace, Dublin 2, D02 AY28, Ireland

BLOOMSBURY, BLOOMSBURY ACADEMIC and the Diana
logo are trademarks of Bloomsbury Publishing Plc

First published in Great Britain 2026

Copyright © Ryan Arthur, 2026

Ryan Arthur has asserted his right under the Copyright,
Designs and Patents Act, 1988, to be identified as Author of this work.

Cover design: Jade Barnett

For legal purposes the Acknowledgements on pp. x–xi
constitute an extension of this copyright page.

All rights reserved. No part of this publication may be: i) reproduced or transmitted in any form, electronic or mechanical, including photocopying, recording or by means of any information storage or retrieval system without prior permission in writing from the publishers; or ii) used or reproduced in any way for the training, development or operation of artificial intelligence (AI) technologies, including generative AI technologies. The rights holders expressly reserve this publication from the text and data mining exception as per Article 4(3) of the Digital Single Market Directive (EU) 2019/790.

Bloomsbury Publishing Plc does not have any control over, or responsibility for, any third-party websites referred to or in this book. All internet addresses given in this book were correct at the time of going to press. The author and publisher regret any inconvenience caused if addresses have changed or sites have ceased to exist, but can accept no responsibility for any such changes.

A catalogue record for this book is available from the British Library.

A catlalog record for this book is available from the Library of Congress.

ISBN: PB: 978-1-3505-1741-7
ePDF: 978-1-3505-1743-1
eBook: 978-1-3505-1742-4

Series: Bloomsbury Study Skills

Typeset by Integra Software Services Pvt. Ltd.

Printed and bound in India

For product safety related questions contact productsafety@bloomsbury.com.

To find out more about our authors and books visit
www.bloomsbury.com and sign up for our newsletters.

In memory of Tom Burns

Contents

Acknowledgements   x
Introduction   xiii

Part 1 Using evidence in your assignment   1

   1 Sources of evidence   3
   2 Referencing and citing   5
   3 Master verbs to help readers follow your line of thought   7
   4 Quoting and paraphrasing   9
   5 State the context of the evidence   11

Part 2 Critical research   13

   6 The search terms hack   15
   7 Use Google Books™ to find definitions of a concept, theory, framework or model   17
   8 Use Google Books™ to find criticisms of a concept, theory, framework, model or scholar   19
   9 Use Google Books™ to find the relationship between two matters   21
  10 The academic book review hack   24
  11 The PhD thesis hack   26
  12 The governmental sources hack   28
  13 'Real-world' information   30
  14 The journal article hack   31

Part 3 How to write an assignment 33

    15 Types of assignments 35
    16 Understanding your assignment task 37
    17 How to write an introduction to your assignment 42
    18 How to write the main body of your assignment 48
    19 How to write a conclusion to your assignment 51

Part 4 How to build arguments 55

    20 Basic argument 57
    21 The however factor 59
    22 There can only be one 63
    23 The middle ground 65
    24 The real world 67
    25 The magic number 70

Part 5 How to critique academic texts 73

    26 Critiquing academic texts using the 'generic' approach 75
    27 Critiquing academic texts using the 'limitations' approach 79
    28 Critiquing academic texts using the 'new' approach 81
    29 Critiquing academic texts using the 'outdated' approach 83
    30 Critiquing academic texts using race, class or gender 85

Part 6 How to incorporate theories, models, concepts and frameworks into your assignment — 87

    31 Incorporating theories, concepts, frameworks and models into your writing — 89
    32 Critiquing models, frameworks, theories and concepts — 96

Part 7 How to reflect critically — 103

    33 Using reflective models to structure your writing — 105
    34 Zooming out to the wider literature — 109
    35 Choosing between two paths — 112
    36 Articulating doubt — 114
    37 Creating themes from your reflection — 117
    38 Bad practice vs best practice — 120
    39 Incorporating statements into your reflection — 122
    40 Incorporating different perspectives into your reflection — 124
    41 Uncovering power in your reflection — 129

Part 8 How to write a dissertation — 133

    42 How to develop a research aim — 135
    43 How to write an introduction — 142
    44 How to write a literature review — 152
    45 How to write a methodology — 165
    46 How to write the findings/results and discussion/analysis chapter — 181
    47 How to write the conclusion chapter — 207
    48 How to write an abstract — 212

Conclusion — 215
Index — 216

Acknowledgements

This book is the result of the collective efforts and support of many individuals whose contributions made this project possible.

I would like to extend my deepest gratitude to my family for their unwavering support. To my wife, Amina, thank you for your constant encouragement and patience. To my children, Farid, Sara, Zach and Maryam, your love and understanding have been a source of strength and inspiration. To my parents, Emmanuel and Tina, your lifelong support and belief in the value of education have shaped who I am today. To my siblings, Tyrone, Siobhan, Leticia and Kevin, your patience and support have been invaluable.

I am grateful to my PhD supervisor, Professor Paul Almond (University of Leicester), who opened the doors of academia to me; all my successes came from this one act. Your belief in my potential and your support at the start of my academic journey laid the foundation for this work. Also, my extended gratitude for those who advocated for me in rooms that I had not yet entered; Angela Ellermeier (Institute for the International Education of Students), Dr Fiona Fisher (University of Warwick), Tom Burns and Sandra Sinfield (London Metropolitan University).

I would also like to thank my colleagues, whose insights, expertise and constructive feedback helped shape the direction and content of this book: Aidan Smith, Joy Igiebor, Harleena Jagde, Nahid Huda, Everton Barton, Kevin Brazant, Dr Uracha Chatrakul Na Ayudhya, Dr Neil Pyper, Dr Mark Stringer, Dr Lisbeth Drury, John Ockey, Dr Charlotte Stevens, Dr Jennie Mills, Dr Jo Kukuczka, Dr Stella Xu, Dr Naif Alghamdi, Anne Halliday and Professor Digby Warren.

Special thanks are due to Helen Caunce and the editorial team, whose guidance and expertise have been essential in bringing this project to fruition.

Finally, I want to acknowledge the thousands of students that I have engaged with. There has been no bigger influence on my pedagogy and the approach of this book than these students. I couldn't possibly name every student and explain how they benefited me; it would take many volumes. I am honoured and grateful to have been given the opportunity to have worked with you all.

To all who have contributed in one way or another, I extend my heartfelt thanks.

The publishers would like to thank the following for permission to reproduce copyright material:

Marrisa Coffey/Noun Project, p. 114; Langtik/Noun Project, p. 114; Arhur Shlain/Noun Project, p. 117; Bernd Lakenbrink/Noun Project, p. 124; Wartini/Noun Project, p. 124; CreationsbyElise/NounProject, p. 124; Chris Homan/Noun Project, p. 136; Icogenix/Noun Project, p. 136; PMSO BEMFEBUNUD/Noun Project, p. 137; Cherry/Noun Project, p. 137; farra nugraha/Noun Project, p. 138; REVA; Noun Project, p. 151; HAJINAIM/Noun Project, p. 180.

Introduction

Welcome to *Ultimate Academic Writing Hacks*! A hack is a clever or unique way of solving a problem or a shortcut to an otherwise lengthy task. These hacks have been developed from my decade-long experience collaborating with students to enhance their academic work. They are tried and tested techniques that can significantly improve the quality of your academic work. Moreover, they are more reliable and quicker to use than artificial intelligence (AI). Some academic departments are hostile to AI use, enforcing strict policies that could lead to penalties. Additionally, AI-generated content raises sustainability and intellectual property concerns, making its use controversial. Therefore, the hacks in this textbook are a viable and less risky alternative.

There are seven matters to be aware of when reading this book.

1 The hacks are malleable

All the hacks in this book are malleable; so, you can adapt, tweak, repurpose, and even combine hacks. Moreover, you are given different options of hacks to suit your particular circumstance. The hacks/approaches should not be seen as the only way; feel free to be creative.

2 The writing style is informal and conversational

Although all the examples are written in academic English, the explanations are written in an informal conversational style. This was done to enhance understanding and achieve a straightforward explanation, so that you can easily find a suitable hack and apply it.

3 You do not have to read this book from beginning to end

The chapters are based on the academic practices that you will need to master. Therefore, you do not have to read this book from beginning to end, you can jump to whichever academic practice you want to master.

4 The examples are summarized

The examples are italicized, summarized and some are colour-coded. The purpose of the examples is to give more clarity to the explanations.

5 The citations are fictitious

Although you can cite this book, most of the citations in the examples are fictitious. However, if the sources are real, you will find the full details of the publications in the corresponding footnotes.

6 Refer to your departmental guidelines

Academic practices and expectations are varied and may differ from context to context. Therefore, your university guidelines and supervisor comments take precedence over the advice of this book. Also, you should review your department's policy on AI.

7 This book provides you with several options

Writing is a multifaceted activity. It takes different forms in each subject area and, even within subject areas, you will find a variety of preferences. Therefore, this book will provide you with several approaches to undertake a particular task; choose the approach that best suits your needs, abilities and subject area requirements.

Part 1

Using evidence in your assignment

What is evidence?

Before you use any hacks/approaches, it is vital to understand how to use evidence to substantiate your ideas, arguments, descriptions and contextual information. This evidence should be relevant, reliable and credible. Constructing evidence-based assignments is crucial for three reasons:

1. It protects you from charges of plagiarism. Plagiarism refers to the act of using someone else's work, ideas or expressions without proper acknowledgement. If you are charged with plagiarism, your assignment is likely to be rejected, or your assignment grade will suffer.
2. It enhances the quality of your assignment. The proper use of evidence will make your assignment impactful and meaningful.
3. It cements your credibility as a genuine academic who understands the importance of basing your ideas on credible and verifiable evidence.

This section will cover five areas:

1. **Sources of evidence**
2. **Referencing and citing**
    Location of in-text citations
    Common mistakes with in-text citations
3. **Master verbs to help readers follow your line of thought**
4. **Quoting and paraphrasing**
    Avoidance of quoting

5. **State the context of the evidence**
   Introduction sentence
   Background information

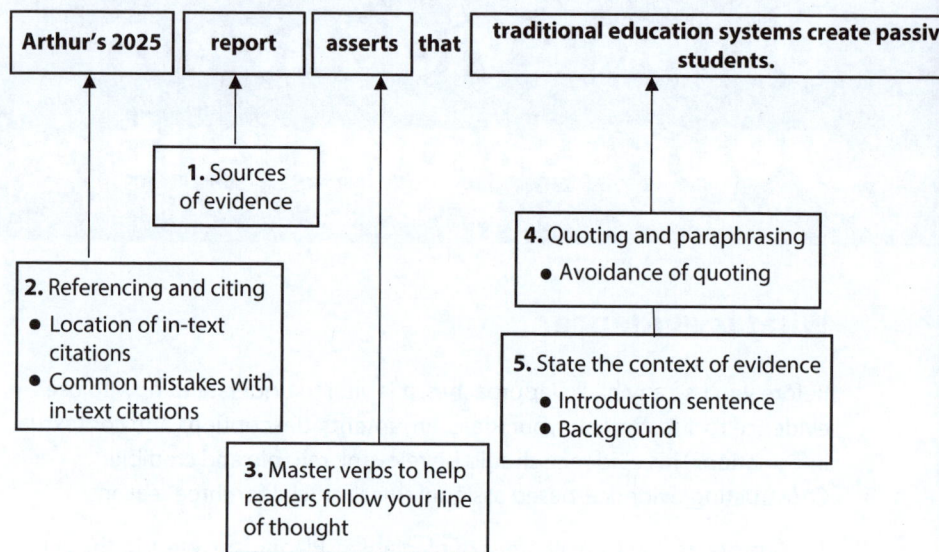

A diagram highlighting the five areas covered in this section

1 Sources of evidence

There are four main reliable and credible sources of evidence to use in your assignments: (1) journal articles, (2) academic books, (3) reports, (4) websites.

1 Journal articles

Journal articles are individual papers written by scholars, researchers, experts and professionals. As the name suggests, journal articles are found in journals; journals are periodical publications that contain a collection of articles on a specific subject or academic field. They are the main platform for scholars, researchers, experts and professionals to share their findings, ideas and developments within a particular subject. When articles are submitted to journals, they undergo a peer review process where they are evaluated and scrutinized by experts before publication to ensure their quality, accuracy and relevance. For such reasons, journal articles are among the best sources of information for your assignments. Journal articles tend to be more current than other sources. Furthermore, journal articles are much shorter than other sources because of their very specific focus.

2 Academic books

There are three main types of books written by scholars or experts. First, single issue books or monographs are detailed studies on a single topic written by one or more authors. They cover topics comprehensively, discussing key issues in great detail. Second, edited volumes are collections of essays or chapters written by different authors, compiled by one or more editors. Edited volumes are great for offering different perspectives on a single theme or topic. The third type is a textbook that is written by one or more authors. They offer comprehensive resources; they cover the main theories, concepts, models and frameworks used in the subject area. They are often used in foundation and undergraduate university courses. They tend to update every few years. Therefore, you should try to use the latest edition.

3 Reports

The third source of information is a report. A report is a document that presents information in an organized format for a very specific audience and purpose. Reports are excellent sources of information; they contain comprehensive data, statistics and analysis on specific topics. You should only use reports that are written by scholars, experts, governmental organizations and well-known and reputable non-governmental organizations. Regarding well-known and reputable non-governmental organizations, they should have a presence and influence beyond the internet, and they try to maintain some degree of neutrality. If you are not sure about the legitimacy of the report, scrutinize the website that hosts the report and google the names of the authors to see who they are. Also, if possible, see who else has cited the report.

4 Websites

The fourth source of information are websites of government agencies and well-known and reputable organizations. Websites provide well-researched, up-to-date and objective information. Reputable websites will host articles, reports, news briefings, policy updates and stakeholder submissions and commentaries that can enhance your assignment. However, not all websites are trustworthy. There are some key signs that indicate the website should be avoided; the website contains advertising of products and services in an intrusive way to the extent that seems to prioritize sales over information. Most reputable websites do not have such overt advertising. Other signs are anonymous authors, non-expert or non-academic authors, lack of citations, information not being updated, noticeable signs of a biased and specific agenda, poor-quality writing, strange or unfamiliar URLs, click bait and misleading or sensational titles. If a webpage shows some of these signs, it's advisable to find a more credible source for your assignment. Reliable sources are backed by identifiable and qualified authors, and reputable organizations.

2 Referencing and citing

Although this section will provide general principles that are useful for most disciplines, please note that there are several referencing styles (APA, MLA, Harvard, etc.) therefore, please refer to your departmental guidelines for specific guidance.

You must state where you found the information to write your assignment. For example, if you mentioned in your assignment that the population of the UK is 67 million, you must state that you found this information on the website of the Office of National Statistics. For every piece of information that comes from outside yourself, you must state the source.

You need to state the source in two places:

1. You need to state it in the body of the assignment; this is called an in-text citation.
2. You need to state it in the reference list at the end of the assignment; this is called a full reference.

1 In-text citation

Imagine that you went to the library and selected this book on the right. You found a passage in the book that you would like to use in your assignment. So, you reword the passage for your assignment. You then add a footnote or in-text citation next to the rewording. The in-text citation is an abbreviation of the book's details; just the author's surname or the organization's name and year it was published in brackets, for example:
(Arthur, 2025) or (Arthur 2025)

2 Full reference

At the end of your assignment, you will write the full reference (name, title of publication, where it was accessed online or where it was published) in the reference list, for example:

Arthur, R. (2025) *Ultimate Academic Writing Hacks*. London: Bloomsbury.

The full reference is placed in the reference list because this is the place to provide the details of all books, articles, reports and webpages you have used in your assignment. When you insert the full reference of the book, article, report or webpage, it should be in alphabetical order. Generally, the reference list is not included in the assignment's overall word count.

Location of in-text citations

Although you can place footnotes almost anywhere in a sentence, in-text citations are restricted to three key places:

1. They can be placed at the beginning of the sentence:

    Example: *Arthur (2025) explains that traditional education systems create passive students, who merely receive, memorize and repeat information without critical thinking.*

2. They can be placed at the end of the sentence:

    Example: *Traditional education systems create passive students, who merely receive, memorize and repeat information without critical thinking (Arthur, 2025).*

3. They can be integrated into the sentence

    Example: *Arthur explains in his 2025 publication that traditional education systems create passive students, who merely receive, memorize and repeat information without critical thinking.*

Common mistakes with in-text citations

- Do not start a sentence with the surname/year or organization/year all in the same brackets. You should start a sentence with author's surname or organization, then put only the year in brackets.

    (Arthur, 2025) explains that … ✗

    Arthur (2025) explains that … ✓

- It is important that you do not add anything inside the brackets other than the author's surname or organization's name and year; do not add initials, URLs, etc.

    (Arthur, R, 2025) (BBC.com, 2025) ✗

    (Arthur, 2025) (BBC, 2025) ✓

- Avoid using the same citation repeatedly; try to diversify your citations to indicate that you have read widely.
- Try to cite as much as possible to demonstrate that you have read widely, at least two citations per paragraph. If you are in doubt whether to cite or not, you should lean towards citing; generally, you will not be penalized for over-citing, but you will be penalized for under-citing.

3 Master verbs to help readers follow your line of thought

A reporting verb is a verb used to indicate that someone is speaking, writing or thinking something. These verbs are used to attribute information, ideas, or opinions to a particular source; this ensures clarity and proper acknowledgement. The reporting verbs are underlined in the examples below:

Keane (2025) states that childhood obesity is increasing.

Campbell (2021) argues that the extended use of social media has a negative impact on mental health.

Lewis (2010) suggests that regular exercise for children improves cognitive function.

Reporting verbs convey different tones. Below is a general guide to help you select the right tone and diversify your use of reporting verbs.

Table 1.1. Table of Reporting Verbs

Tone	Reporting verb	Example
Stating a fact or something is commonly known	Says States Reports Describes Mentions	Keane (2025) states that childhood obesity is increasing
Put forward a claim or an argument	Argues Claims Asserts Contends Insists	Kent (2021) argues that education reform has been limited
Make a suggestion	Suggests Proposes Recommends Puts forward Offers	Palmer (2019) proposes a new pedagogy to address current inequalities

To show agreement	Agrees Supports Endorses Confirms Corroborates	*Sanchez (2019) corroborates Smith's (2010) approach*
Provide an explanation	Explains Clarifies Interprets Expounds Describes	*Cann (2022) explains the process of recidivism*
To show disagreement	Disagrees Refutes Rejects Challenges Contradicts	*Brown (2018) refutes the claim that globalization is beneficial to the global south*
Something is questionable	Questions Doubts Criticizes Queries Casts doubt	*The author casts doubt on the validity of the government's figures*
Emphasize a point	Emphasizes Highlights Stresses Underlines Points out	*The author highlights the importance of foundation programmes*
To show something	Shows Demonstrate Illustrates Reveals Indicates	*The data reveals that school expulsions have increased over the decade*

4 Quoting and Paraphrasing

Quoting and paraphrasing are two ways to incorporate the ideas or words of others into your work. Quoting is when you copy the exact words that someone else has said or written. The quoted words are typically enclosed in quotation marks, and the author or organization, year of publication and page of source are cited. For example:

(Ivanov, 2026, p. 23) or (Ivanov, 2026, p.23)

In contrast, paraphrasing or rewording is when you express the meaning of someone else's words using your own words. For example:

Original text	Your rewording
We can confidently date the end of the Cold War to 1991 with the dissolution of the Warsaw Pact.	Morrison (2014) mentions that the Cold War ended in 1991, marked by the dissolution of the Warsaw Pact.

When you paraphrase, it is vital that you do not overcomplicate or obscure the original meaning of the text.

Avoidance of quoting

You should only quote if you are instructed to, the phrasing is incredibly distinct or perhaps the text describes an idea so clearly and eloquently that you want to capture the exact words. Nonetheless, it is better to paraphrase for three reasons. First, it indicates to the marker that you have a good understanding of the topic. Articulating someone else's words in your own words requires understanding, whereas cutting and pasting text into your assignment does not. Second, quoting increases your similarity rating. A high similarity rating can lead to charges of plagiarism. When you submit an assignment, it will be automatically scanned by software to see how similar your assignment is to other work that has been submitted and published. Generally, paraphrasing will protect you against high similarity rates. Third, paraphrasing does not have as many rules as quoting. For example, if you quote from a publication, you need to add quotation marks and include the page number of the publication. Additionally, if the passage that you are quoting is more than forty words or two sentences you need to separate the quote from the rest of the paragraph, indent the quote, then place the colon before the indented quote, etc. As you can see, there are so many rules. Whereas paraphrasing has only two simple rules:

1. You need to reword someone else's words while retaining their original meaning. Your paraphrasing does not have to be 100 per cent different from the original; you can use a few words from the original.
2. You need to add a citation next to the rewording and write the full reference at the end of your assignment.

5 State the context of the evidence

Before you paraphrase or quote someone else's work, it is always good to provide some context *before* the quote or paraphrase. Context is background information. There are two approaches to providing context: (1) an introduction sentence, (2) background.

1 An introduction sentence

An introduction sentence is the opening sentence of a paragraph. It makes explicit the main idea that your paraphrases and quotes are trying to get across; whatever you want your quotes or paraphrases to indicate it should be stated in the introduction sentence. When we do not include an introduction sentence, we make it much harder for the reader to understand our intent of using a particular quote or paraphrase. For example, a student paraphrased the sentence below from a passage in Johnson's 2021 article.

Women earned on average £13.99 per hour, compared to male employees who earned £15.48 per hour (Johnson, 2021). 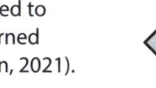	This example sentence is not a good way to start a paragraph, it requires an introduction sentence to give us more clarity.
There is a disparity between how men and women are paid. Women earned on average £13.99 per hour, compared to male employees who earned £15.48 per hour (Johnson, 2021).	By adding this introduction sentence, we have shown our intent of using Johnson's study. Avoid starting a paragraph with a quote, paraphrase or data, always start with an introduction sentence.

2 Background

Occasionally, add some background information to the passage that you have paraphrased or quoted to demonstrate that you have read widely. Adding background information indicates that you are aware of the scholar that you are quoting or paraphrasing. For example:

Choeying (2021) found that plagiarism has been dealt with more punitively in UK universities since the move to online learning.	This example sentence is without any background information.
Through her documentary analysis of academic integrity policies from 18 universities, Choeying (2021) found that plagiarism has been dealt with more punitively in UK universities since the move to online learning.	By adding just a few words of background information, you have demonstrated that you have intimate knowledge of Choeying's work; this is not just a random text that you have paraphrased, but it is something that you have read fully.

By adding a few words of background information, you can demonstrate awareness of the intellectual tradition or biography of the individual that you are quoting or paraphrasing. For example:

Freire (1974, p. 24) asserted that, 'Leaders who do not act dialogically do not organize the people – they manipulate them.'

This example sentence is without any background information.

Freire (1974, p. 24), a leading advocate of critical pedagogy, asserted that, 'Leaders who do not act dialogically do not organize the people – they manipulate them.'

By adding a few words of background information about the author, you have demonstrated knowledge that goes beyond the text. Here are some other examples:

Ellsworth, a post structural feminist, argues that …

Simeon who has a background in sports science stated …

Jones, an American professor of public health, contends that …

It is especially impactful to mention the author's background, if they are writing in a different field from their typical field.

Additionally, by adding a few words of background information, you are demonstrating that you know the wider context around the work you have paraphrased or quoted. For example:

Farid (2021) argues that there is no single best culture for all organizations.

This example sentence is without any background information.

In reaction to Peters and Waterman's 2020 article on organizational conformity, Farid (2021) argues that there is no single best culture for all organizations.

By adding a few words of background information, you have demonstrated your awareness of the context around Farid's work. Scholarly work does not exist in a vacuum, it is a reaction to what came before it and events of that period. This all can be acknowledged with just a few background words.

Part 2

Critical research

Critical research hacks

Critical research skills are fundamental for academic success. They enable you to manipulate search engines, databases or online catalogues to locate relevant and informative sources. This section will present nine ways of finding information to enhance your assignments.

6. The search terms hack
7. Use Google Books™ to find definitions of a concept, theory, framework or model.
8. Use Google Books™ to find criticisms of a concept, theory, framework, model or scholar
9. Use Google Books™ to find the relationship between two matters
10. The academic book review hack
11. The PhD thesis hack
12. The government sources hack
13. The 'real-world' information hack
14. The journal article hack

Follow the step-by-step methods of these guides to find information quickly. These approaches are open to new ideas, so feel free to add, omit, merge or tweak to suit your needs.

6 | The search terms hack

Critical research is reliant on creating search terms from the words of your assignment question. You can create search terms by placing the words of your assignment question into three categories: command words, topic words and restrictive words. Below is an example of placing the words of your assignment question into three categories:

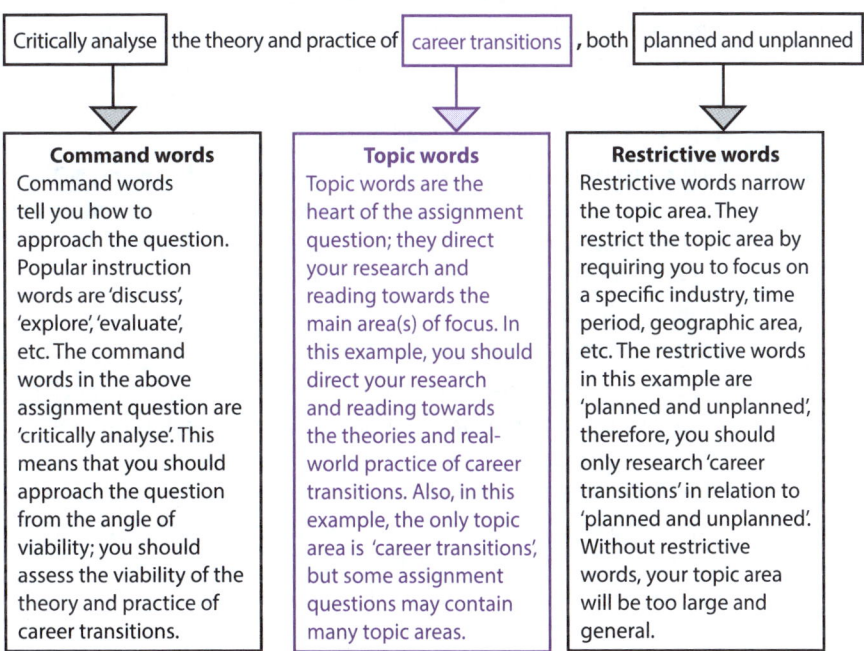

Command words	Topic words	Restrictive words
Command words tell you how to approach the question. Popular instruction words are 'discuss', 'explore', 'evaluate', etc. The command words in the above assignment question are 'critically analyse'. This means that you should approach the question from the angle of viability; you should assess the viability of the theory and practice of career transitions.	Topic words are the heart of the assignment question; they direct your research and reading towards the main area(s) of focus. In this example, you should direct your research and reading towards the theories and real-world practice of career transitions. Also, in this example, the only topic area is 'career transitions', but some assignment questions may contain many topic areas.	Restrictive words narrow the topic area. They restrict the topic area by requiring you to focus on a specific industry, time period, geographic area, etc. The restrictive words in this example are 'planned and unplanned', therefore, you should only research 'career transitions' in relation to 'planned and unplanned'. Without restrictive words, your topic area will be too large and general.

After you categorize the words of your assignment question into command words, topic words and restrictive words, type the topic words and restrictive words into a search engine, database or online catalogue to get the best search results.

If you are still not getting relevant search results, use Boolean operators to enhance the relevancy of the search results. Boolean operators are words and symbols that can be used in almost every search engine, database or online catalogue to specify your search results.

Table 2.1 Boolean operators

AND	Combine your search terms with **AND** to make sure that they all appear in your search results. For example, searching for 'fake news **AND** media' will make sure your results contain all these terms.
OR	Using **OR** in your search combines synonyms. For example, typing 'teenagers **OR** adolescents' finds results that contain either 'teenagers or adolescents'. This widens your search net. If you type 'teenagers' alone, only articles containing 'teenagers' will appear, you will not see articles that use the term 'adolescents' instead of 'teenagers'.
NOT	Using **NOT** in your search will exclude the word following **NOT**. For example, if you type 'Psychology **NOT** Developmental', results that contain the word 'psychology' will appear in your results list, but results that also contain the word 'developmental' will be excluded. This is a great way to exclude concepts that may be implied by your search terms.
" "	Quotation marks are used when you are searching for a specific word combination or an exact phrase. Some search terms are better expressed as a specific word combination or an exact phrase to improve the precision of your search. For example, if you did a search for professional communication, and you didn't use quotation marks, you will receive all results that have the words 'professional' and 'communication' individually, making your results list much longer and less relevant. When you use quotation marks, you filter the search results, ensuring that you only receive results with the term 'professional communication'.

7 Use Google Books™ to find definitions of a concept, theory, framework or model

This hack will show you how to use Google Books™ to find relevant information for your assessment. Google Books™ is a free digital database that requires no login, and there is no paywall. Google Books™ has scanned millions of publications into its database. When you type a search term into Google Books™, it will search through the text of millions of publications. It will take you to the exact page of your search term and even highlight the exact paragraph. Even though Google Books™ will only show you a preview (two to three pages) of the book, this should be enough to get the information you need. If not, you can obtain the physical book from your university library.

This hack is useful for retrieving definitions of topic words, concepts, theories, frameworks and models from academic sources. In order to achieve higher grades, your definitions should be derived from academic sources rather than from dictionaries or your own thoughts.

Step one Go to the Google Books™ homepage – the website address for Google Books™ is books.google.co.uk, or you can type Google Books into the Google search engine.	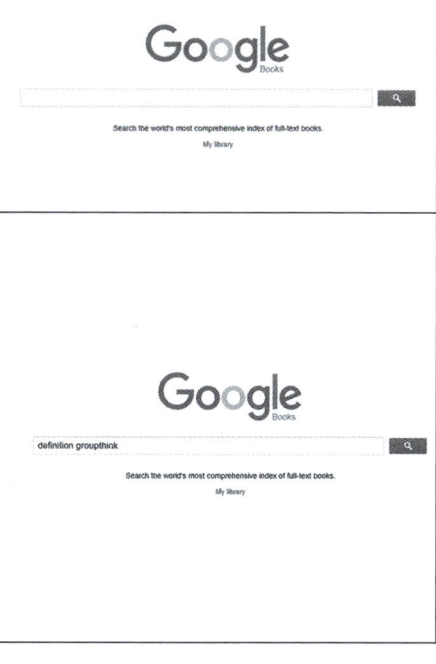
Step two In the Google Books™ search bar, type the word 'definition' along with the name of the theory, concept, model or framework that you want to define. Google Books™ will scan through millions of books to look for definitions for that theory, model, framework or concept. In the adjacent example, a student is using Google Books™ to find a definition for 'groupthink'.	

Continued...

17

Continued...

Step three

Near the top of the page you will find several search options. Click **Any view**, then select **Preview** and **Full view**. You should select **Preview** and **Full view** because you only want to see books with a preview or full view. Additionally, click on **Any document,** then select **Books** because you only want to see books. If you cannot see these search options, click on the **Tools** icon, and then they should appear. If you still cannot see these search options, do not worry, the hack will still work. These search options merely limit the search results to make it easier to find what you need.

Step four

You should see a list of search results. All these search results are books that contain definitions of groupthink. However, only click on search results that state, **Found inside – page number**. This is because you only want search results that take you to the exact page. When you click on your desired search result, scroll to the top of the book to retrieve the referencing information.

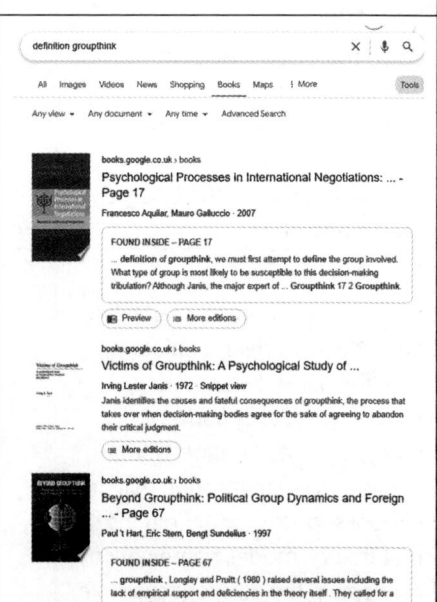

8 Use Google Books™ to find criticisms of a concept, theory, framework, model or scholar

This hack will give you the confidence to criticize topic words, concepts, theories, frameworks, models and even scholars. Additionally, to achieve higher grades, you must include criticisms. Google Books™ is an excellent database of scholarly criticisms.

Step one	
Go to the Google Books™ homepage. The website address for Google Books™ is books.google.co.uk, or you can type Google Books into the Google search engine.	
Step two	
In the Google Books™ search bar, type the word 'criticism' or 'criticisms' or 'critic' or 'critics' along with the name of the theory, concept, model or framework that you want to criticize. Google Books™ will scan through millions of books to look for scholarly criticisms for that theory, model, framework or concept. In the adjacent example, a student is using Google Books™ to find a criticism for groupthink.	

Continued...

Continued...

Step three

Near the top of the page you will find several search options. Click **Any view**, then select **Preview** and **Full view**. You should select Preview and Full view because you only want to see books with a preview or full view. Additionally, click on **Any document**, then select **Books** because you only want to see books. If you cannot see these search options, click on the **Tools** icon, and then they should appear. If you still cannot see these search options, do not worry, the hack will still work. These search options merely limit the search results to make it easier to find what you need.

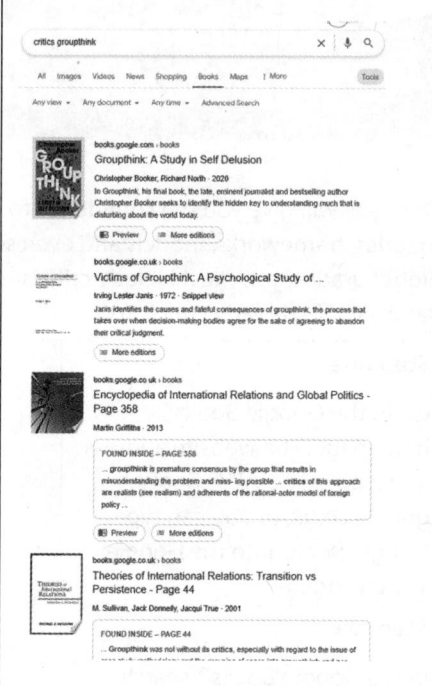

Step four

You should see a list of search results. All these search results are books that contain criticisms of groupthink. However, only click on search results that state, **Found inside – page number**. This is because you only want search results that take you to the exact page. When you click on your desired search result, scroll to the top of the book to retrieve the referencing information.

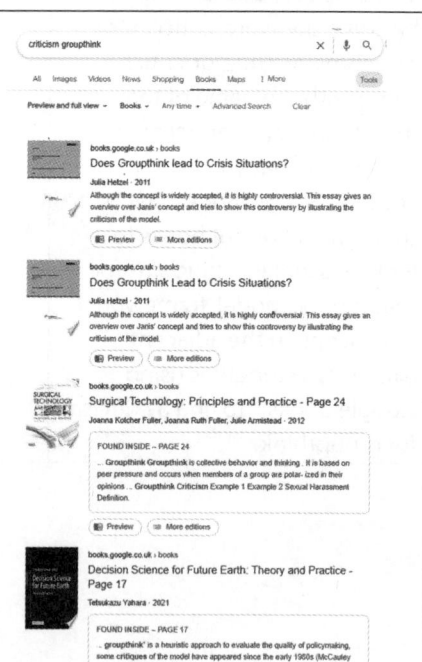

9 Use Google Books™ to find the relationship between two matters

This hack will show you what scholars have written about two matters that you are interested in. You may want to know the relationship between two periods (Covid-19 and post-Covid-19) or the similarities and differences between two scholars (Foucault and Sartre) or two theories (Critical theory and social constructivism), or if a particular methodology was used to research a particular subject (critical realism and marketing) or how a scholar was received in a particular part of the world (Marx and France). There are numerous combinations to try; experiment with different formulations to get the best results.

Step one	
Go to the Google Books™ homepage – the website address for Google Books™ is books.google.co.uk, or you can type Google Books into the Google search engine.	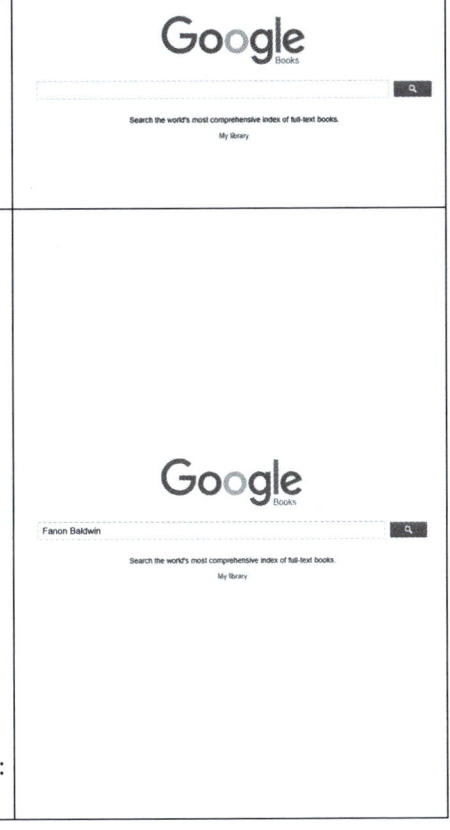
Step two	
In the Google Books™ search bar, type the word or scholar's name along with the word or scholar's name. Google Books™ will scan through millions of books to search for books that mention these two words, two names or two periods. If you are looking for a scholar, type their surname (Freire) or their full name in between speech marks ("Paulo Freire"). In the adjacent example, a student is using Google Books™ to find studies that discuss the relationship between two scholars: James Baldwin and Frantz Fanon.	

Continued...

Continued...

Step three

Near the top of the page you will find several search options. Click **Any view**, then select **Preview** and **Full view**. You should select Preview and Full view because you only want to see books with a preview or full view. Additionally, click on **Any document**, then select **Books** because you only want to see books. If you cannot see these search options, click on the **Tools** icon, and then they should appear. If you still cannot see these search options, do not worry, the hack will still work. These search options merely limit the search results to make it easier to find what you need.

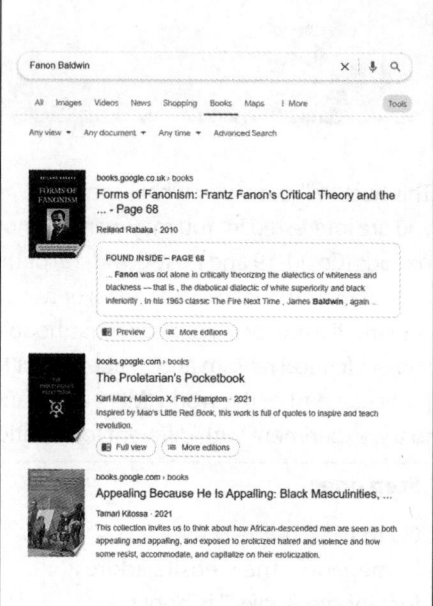

Step four

You should see a list of search results. All these search results are books that contain the two words or two names. However, only click on search results that state, **Found inside – page number**. This is because you only want search results that take you to the exact page. When you click on your desired search result, scroll to the top of the book to retrieve the referencing information.

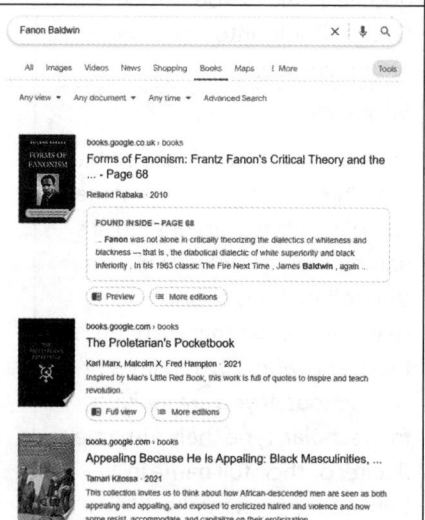

General tips for using Google Books™

- Most books on Google Books™ are legitimate and trustworthy. However, if you are unsure, visit the WorldCat website (https://search.worldcat.org). WorldCat.org is a global catalogue of library materials. If your book is listed on WorldCat, it is a legitimate publication.

- If you are unable to find what you are looking for on page 1 of the search results, keep scrolling through the pages. Additionally, do not be afraid to experiment and enhance the hack to get the best results.

- If you are unable to find a page that has criticism of a model, concept, theory or concept, then add more information to your search. For example, if you are type in: *criticism Lewin model*, and you not able to find any criticisms of Lewin's model, then add more information to your search: *criticism Lewin model freezing unfreezing*. 'Freezing' and 'unfreezing' are essential stages in Lewin's model.

- While scrolling through the pages of a book, if you come across this message

    You have either reached a page that is unavailable for viewing or reached your viewing limit for this book.

    on a page, **'You have either reached a page that is unavailable for viewing or reached your viewing limit for this book',** then scroll past this page, wait a few seconds, then scroll back, you should now have access to the page.

10 The academic book review hack

Using academic book reviews can significantly enhance your learning and academic writing. Academic book reviews are journal articles that evaluate books written by academics. Academic book reviews are usually written for academic audiences and are mainly published in peer-reviewed academic journals. Academic book reviews can help you in four ways:

1. Academic book reviews are an excellent shortcut to mastering your required reading. In most universities, students are required to read a list of publications on a weekly basis. If you do not have the time to read each book in the list, you can read reviews of the book to get an overview of the book's purpose, scope, context and main arguments. Since book reviews are typically one to five pages, they are a quick way to obtain well-rounded, expert perspectives on the books you are studying.

2. Academic book reviews will provide you with a critical evaluation of theories, models, frameworks and concepts. Most contemporary theories, models, frameworks and concepts that you will study at university started life in a journal article, then later evolved into a book. Thus, a book review will usually contain a critique of theories, models, frameworks and concepts.

3. Academic book reviews will provide you with important contextual information. Reviews will often discuss what the book is reacting to, how the book contributes to ongoing academic discussions and provides insight into its intellectual tradition.

4. Academic book reviews will provide you with research guidance by highlighting knowledge gaps and suggestions of further readings or related works.

How to find academic book reviews

Academic book reviews can be obtained from two sources:

1. The first source is your university's library online search engine. As a student, you will be given full access to your university's library service.
    - Type in the book's name; most academic reviews will contain the name of the book in its title.
    - For more accurate results place the book's title in between speech marks, for example, "Britain and the Aftermath of Empire".

- Narrow your search to 'journals', 'journal articles', 'articles', 'online resources', 'online items', etc. However, if your university's library online search engine does not allow you to narrow your search, it should still display links to book reviews.

- Some universities' library search engines will allow you to narrow your search even further by giving you the options to search for just 'book reviews'.

2. The second source is an online academic journal repository, such as JSTOR, SpringerLink, Sage Journals, Wiley Online Library, etc. Most online academic journal repositories have a paywall. However, you should be able to gain access via an institutional login option.

    - Type in the book's name; most academic reviews will contain the name of the book in its title.

    - For more accurate results place the book's title in between speech marks, for example, "Britain and the Aftermath of Empire".

    - Some journal repositories will allow you to narrow your search to just 'book reviews'.

If you cannot find an academic book review from the above two sources, try to search for it in Google or other mainstream search engines. Though rare, it is possible that some academic book reviews are not accessible through your university search engine or your chosen journal repository. Additionally, Google and other mainstream search engines may locate some academic book reviews that are hosted on the websites of well-known public-facing organizations and well-established periodicals. Reviews found on these sites can be used as peripheral sources of evidence.

11 The PhD thesis hack

Unfortunately, some students believe that a PhD thesis is too complicated for them to use. This is generally not true. A PhD thesis is an original piece of research which can be a beneficial source of information for your university assessments. There are three reasons why you should use a PhD thesis:

1. PhD theses offer cutting-edge findings and unique perspectives that are rarely found in other sources This is because the primary goal of a PhD thesis is to contribute original research and insights to their field.
2. The depth of research in a typical PhD thesis is not matched by a journal article. Articles are relatively short compared to a PhD thesis.
3. A PhD thesis from a recognized university is a credible source because it underwent supervision, scrutiny and rigorous review by experts in the field.

How to use a PhD thesis

Gain an overview of the entire subject by just reading select pages:
Most PhD theses contain a 'literature review' section or chapter. A literature review is a comprehensive summary and critical analysis of the existing research on a particular topic. By reading the literature review, you will acquire an understanding of the subject's contextual factors, chronological development of the subject area, controversies and areas of minimal research. You will also learn about the central thinkers, theories, models, concepts and frameworks.

Learn how to develop a methodology for your dissertation/project:
Most PhD theses contain a 'methodology' section or chapter. The methodology chapter in a PhD thesis outlines the research design and methods used to collect and analyse data. This can be very useful if you are having trouble developing the methodology for your dissertation/project. Most methodologies in journal articles are too short to provide an example of a methodology, whereas PhD methodology sections are long enough to not only give you an example, but you can replicate the research method for your own dissertation.

Locate key sources of information: A PhD thesis contains an extensive bibliography. Therefore, if you are having trouble finding information about a particular topic, you can peruse the PhD thesis's bibliography to find relevant sources.

Contact the author: To gain more insight into a subject, why not contact the author of the PhD thesis? Those who complete PhDs are likely to have public contact information via the institution that employs them or sites like LinkedIn. Many will be happy to discuss their thesis with someone that has read it, as it was their passion project for several years and they may not have had much opportunity to discuss it in their present roles.

Searching for a PhD thesis

When searching for a PhD thesis, the title of the thesis does not have to exactly match your area of interest. For example, if you are searching for a thesis on Corporate Social Responsibility in the UK, but you find a thesis titled 'CSR in Brazil', this thesis can still be helpful. This is because a PhD thesis will usually start in a general way, then gradually narrow its focus. For example, the beginning of the 'CSR in Brazil' PhD thesis will most likely contain general information on CSR's central thinkers, definitions and also the theories, models, concepts and frameworks associated with CSR, all of which will be useful to your UK study. A general rule is that a thesis will contain information on a general concept, then it will gradually focus on a specific area (geographic area, specific industry, time period, etc.)

Table 2.2 Finding a PhD thesis

Database	Description
British Library's EThOS	A repository for UK PhD theses
Open Access Theses and Dissertations	Open access postgraduate theses and dissertations published around the world
DART-Europe: e-theses portal	DART-Europe is a database of European doctoral theses and some masters dissertations
Networked Digital Library of Theses and Dissertations (NDLTD).	For a country-by-country list of PhD repositories, please refer to https://ndltd.org/thesis-resources/find-etds/

12 The governmental sources hack

This hack will help you locate government data. Your assessments could benefit from government data in several ways:

- **Identifying the prevalence:** Government information often contains data about the prevalence of an issue. If you claim that there is a problem, you will need to substantiate your claim with data that indicates the prevalence of a problem. For example, if you claim that childhood obesity is a problem, you will need to provide data on the prevalence of childhood obesity.
- **Providing up-to-date information:** Whereas articles and books contain information about past events, government databases reveal the most current information.
- **Indicating the significance of your assignment:** Whenever you convey information, it is important to highlight the significance of the information. You can evidence the significance of your information by referring to current government action to ameliorate or address the particular situation.

Table 2.3 How to find government information

Database	Description
GOV.UK https://www.gov.uk/	Search engine for governmental information and services. You can narrow your search results by **content type** and **topic**.
Policy papers and consultations https://www.gov.uk/search/policy-papers-and-consultations	A repository of governmental policy papers and consultations. You can narrow your **topic, document type, organization world location** and **date**.
Open data https://www.data.gov.uk/	A repository of data published by central government, local authorities and public bodies.

Hansard https://hansard.parliament.uk/	Hansard is a report of what is said in Parliament. You can find Members, their contributions, debates, petitions and divisions from published Hansard reports, dating back over 200 years.
Committee https://committees.parliament.uk/publications/	Find information on government committees including their inquiries and publications. Government committees consider policy issues, scrutinize government work, expenditure, and examine proposals for primary and secondary legislation.

Alternatively, you can perform a Google search, type UK government and your area of interest in the search bar. For example, **UK government + artificial intelligence**.

uk government artificial intelligence

13 'Real-world' information

In academia, 'real-world information' refers to data and knowledge derived from practical, real-life contexts rather than theoretical or simulated environments. If possible, try to incorporate 'real-world' information into your assignments. This will demonstrate to the marker that you can bring together academic theory and real-world practice. Using real-world information will add 'flesh' to your assessments and separate you from other students.

Emerald Insight™ (https://www.emerald.com/insight/) is a brilliant and trustworthy resource to gather real-world information. You can gather real-world information via two routes:

1. **Professional perspectives:** Emerald Insight™ contains expert briefings, books and articles written by professional organizations, professionals and experts. Professional perspectives can complement your academic sources of information to give a more rounded view.

2. **Case studies:** Emerald Insight™ also provides case studies. A case study is an in-depth examination of a specific subject, such as a person, group, event, industry/sector or organization, within its real-world context.

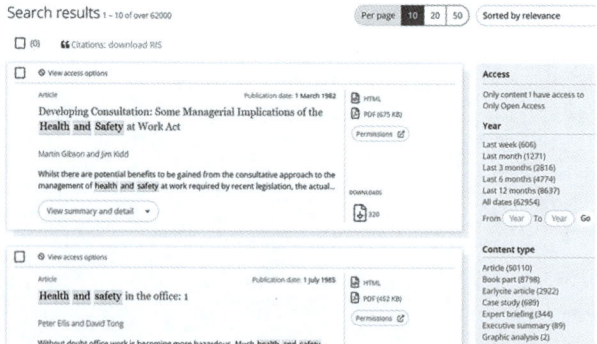

If you are interested in a particular person, group, event, industry/sector or organization, type the name of the person, group, event, industry/sector or organization into the search bar and narrow the search results to **Case studies**. Alternatively, if you are interested in a case study that relates to a particular theory, model, concepts or framework, type it the name of the theory, model, concepts or framework in the search bar, then narrow the search results to **Case studies**.

14 The journal article hack

Generally, journal articles are considered the best source of information (refer to page 3 for more information on journal articles). You can find reliable journal articles via your university library database or refer to Table 2.4 below. Most articles are behind a paywall. However, your university will automatically provide you with **institutional access**:

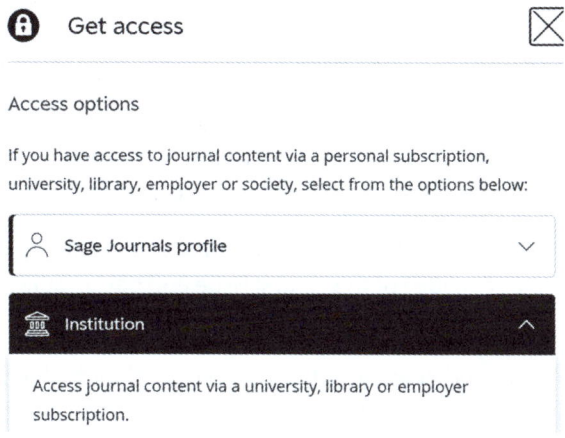

Table 2.4 Journal repositories

Name of journal repository	Description
Sage Journals https://journals.sagepub.com/	Sage Journals has a portfolio of more than 1,100 journals, including over 200 gold open access journals, and 400 society partners.
Taylor & Francis Online https://www.tandfonline.com/	Taylor & Francis Online houses over 2,700 journals, including the world's largest programme of Social Science and Humanities journals, theoretical and applied Science, Technology and Medicine content.

Springer Nature Link https://link.springer.com/	Springer hosts a wide portfolio of journals, over 3,000, which cover the full range of research disciplines.
JSTOR https://www.jstor.org/	JSTOR provides access to more than 12 million journal articles, books, images and primary sources in 75 disciplines.
Wiley Online Library https://onlinelibrary.wiley.com/	Wiley has a portfolio of over 8 million articles from 1,600 journals that cover life, health and physical sciences, social science and the humanities.

You can gain an understanding from journal articles by reading key sections.

Step one: Read the abstract of the journal article, in just a few hundred words, the abstract will provide you with a concise overview of the study, including its purpose, methods, key findings and implications.

Step two: If the abstract information is relevant to you, then read the introduction to get an idea of the central issue and background information.

Step three: Go to the discussion section or the section after the results/findings to understand how the author(s) interpret their findings and see the connections between results and prior research.

Step four: Review the conclusion section for a summary of the key points.

Step five: Scan the bibliography/reference list for sources that might be useful for further reading.

Part 3

How to write an assignment

How to write an assignment

This section will guide you through the steps to write a compelling and exceptional assignment. Each step plays a crucial role in the overall quality of your work. In order to provide you with a structured approach to present your ideas clearly and convincingly, this part will cover five areas:

15. Types of assignments

16. Understanding your assignment task

17. How to write an introduction to your assignment

18. How to write the main body to your assignment

19. How to write a conclusion to your assignment

By the end of this chapter, you will be equipped with the knowledge and skills necessary to tackle university assignments with full confidence.

15 Types of assignments

A university assignment is a task or project given to you to assess your understanding of the subject matter, your ability to apply concepts learned in lectures and readings, and your aptitude in critical thinking, research and writing.

There are four main types of assignments: essays, reports, presentations and reflections. Although there are newer forms of assessments, many will contain some of the core requirements of the four main types. All other assignments are variations of these four types. Therefore, if you get an assignment that you are not sure about, you can ask your lecturer: 'Is it like an essay? Is it like a report? Is it like a presentation? or Is it like a reflection?'

Table 3.1 Different types of assignments

Types of assignments	Description
Essay	An essay articulates your perspective on a particular topic. Your perspective needs to be presented objectively. This means that you should avoid using words and terms that are emotive and indicate bias. Although you are putting forward a perspective, you must present yourself as an impartial observer. Thus, you must avoid personal pronouns (I, you, my) and speak in the third person; for example, instead of saying, 'my essay will' you should say, 'this essay will'. An essay is also discursive, which means that although you are putting forward a perspective, you must show a 'back and forth' between the perspective you are advocating and perspectives that contrast with it.
Report	A report is a detailed account of an event, situation, product, approach, options available or research findings. Your account needs to be presented objectively. This means that you should avoid using words and terms that are emotive and indicate bias. You must present yourself as an impartial observer. Thus, you must avoid personal pronouns (I, we, you, my, our) and speak in the third person; for example, instead of saying, 'my report will'

	you should say, 'this report will'. Unlike an essay, a report is not discursive, you do not need to show a 'back and forth' between perspectives. Instead, you are heading forwards in one direction and only highlighting evidence to advance your account, instead of showing evidence just to get into a debate. Imagine that you are handing this report to your busy manager. She does not want to see a 'back-and-forth' discursive debate. She wants to see a clear account and the clear articulation of how the evidence supports your account.
Presentation	An oral presentation is a form of public speaking where students present their research, proposition or findings to an audience. These presentations can be done individually or as part of a group and often involve the use of visual aids like PowerPoint slides. You need to present your information objectively. This means that you should avoid using words and terms that are emotive and indicate bias. However, there is some flexibility over the use of personal pronouns. A presentation is not as discursive as an essay; you do not need to show too much 'back and forth' between perspectives. Instead, you are generally heading forwards in one direction and only seeking to advance your proposition with evidence. Imagine that you are delivering this presentation to your team at work. They do not want to see a 'back-and-forth' discursive debate. They want to see a clear articulation of your research, proposition or findings and how the evidence supports it.
Reflection	A reflection at university is a process where students critically analyse their experiences, considering what they have learned, how they have changed, and how these experiences might influence their future actions. Reflections may be in an essay format, oral presentation or a journal. You are encouraged to present reflective accounts subjectively. You are not an impartial observer; you are an active participant.

16 Understanding your assignment task

There are four approaches to understanding the assignment task. You can use whichever approach is relevant, or you can combine them.

Approach 1: Sort the assignment task into three categories

A typical assignment task can be sorted into three categories: **command words**, **topic words** and **restrictive words**.

Critically analyse the theory and practice of career transitions, both planned and unplanned.

Command words in an assignment task are usually verbs that guide the structure and focus of your assignment. They direct you to respond to the assignment task in a particular way. See Table 3.2 for some common command words.

Topic words are the heart of the assignment task. They indicate the main subject or area that you need to focus on. These words help you understand what the assignment is about and guide your research and writing. For example, in the assignment task: *Critically analyse the theory and practice of career transitions, both planned and unplanned*, the topic words are *career transitions*. The topic words direct you to focus on career transitions.

Restrictive words are terms that limit the scope of your response, guiding you to focus on a specific aspect of a topic. Be mindful of restrictive words to ensure that your answer is precise and relevant to what is being asked. Restrictive words can limit your assignment to a specific time frame, particular location, specific population, or an aspect, such as 'planned and unplanned'.

Table 3.2. Command words

Command words	Definition
Account for	Like 'explain', but with a focus on the reasons why something is the way it is or why it did not develop in a particular way.
Analyse/critically analyse	Break down the topic into parts, then examine each part.
Apply	Put something to use, show how something can be used in a particular situation.
Assess	Offer a reasoned judgement of the quality, value or importance of something, or weigh up if it meets a particular standard.
Compare	Identify similarities and differences between two or more subjects.
Contrast	Focus on the differences between two or more subjects.
Criticize/critique	Identify the strengths and weaknesses of something and give your judgement about the merit.
Define	Provide the meaning of a given term. If possible, give more than one view on the term's meaning.
Develop	Take forward to a more advanced stage or build upon given information.
Devise	Work out a plan, solve a problem, etc.
Discuss	Explore the topic in detail, considering examples, different perspectives and arguments.
Evaluate/ critically evaluate	Judge the value or significance of something, considering both strengths and weaknesses.
Examine	Focus on something and question it where appropriate.
Explain	Make something clear by describing it in more detail and provide examples. If possible, reveal issues that may be implicit.
Illustrate	Make clear and explicit; usually requires the use of examples.
Justify	Provide reasons/evidence to support something.
Outline	Set out the main points.
Relate	Show how certain things are connected or affect each other or show to what extent they are alike.

Review	Examine something closely. Usually, this means concluding with your own judgement as to its strength.
State	Express clearly.
Suggest	Apply knowledge and understanding to situations in order to make proposals or put forward considerations.
Summarize	Give a concise, clear explanation or account of something, presenting the main factors and excluding minor details.
Support	Give reasons/evidence/examples for something.
Synthesize	Merge two or more things together and assess their compatibility.
To what extent …	Consider how far something is true and how convincing the evidence is.

Approach 2: Turn your assignment task into a 'yes, no or maybe' question

You can simplify your assignment task by turning it into a question that can be responded to with Yes, No or Maybe. Although this does not work with every assignment task, it is an effective way to simplify the assignment task, satisfy the marker and give your assignment a strong narrative.

For example, you can respond with **Yes, No or Maybe** to this assignment task:

Examine the role of social media in shaping contemporary political movements transforms into a question: *Does social media have a role in shaping contemporary political movements?*

Yes: If you believe that the answer to this assignment task is 'yes', then the majority of the assignment should indicate why and how social media has a role in shaping contemporary political movements. You will use examples, theories, case studies, scholarly opinions and so on, to prove that social media has a role in shaping contemporary political movements. Although you will mention contrasting views, it should be clear throughout the assignment that you are affirming that social media has a role in shaping contemporary political movements.

No: If you believe that the answer to this assignment task is 'no', then the majority of the assignment should indicate why and how social media does **not** have a role in shaping contemporary political movements. You will use examples, theories, case studies, scholarly opinions, etc., to prove that social media does **not** have a role in shaping contemporary political movements.

Although you will mention contrasting views, it should be clear throughout the assignment that you are affirming that social media does **not** have a role in shaping contemporary political movements.

Maybe: You may want to respond with a 'maybe'. You will argue that the matter is too unclear to know with certainty. Then most of the assignment should indicate why social media's role in shaping contemporary political movements is a convoluted issue. You will use examples, theories, case studies, scholarly opinions, etc., to prove that social media's role in shaping contemporary political movements is an issue without a clear answer. This may involve mentioning disagreement, lack of consensus and for and against perspectives that annul each other.

Alternatively, your 'maybe' position may argue that certain circumstances/conditions need to be present before there can be a 'yes' or a 'no'. Then, most of the assignment should indicate what these circumstances/conditions are and why this is so. You will use examples, theories, case studies, scholarly opinions, etc., to prove that these circumstances/conditions are absolutely necessary for social media to have a role in shaping contemporary political movements.

Approach 3: Issue-by-issue

This approach is for assignment tasks that require you to address two or more topic words. To see what this approach looks like in practice, I will breakdown this assignment task:

> **Discuss the role of fiscal and monetary policies in addressing economic inequality.**

Approach this assignment task issue-by-issue. Break it down into manageable chunks. Otherwise, if you address multiple issues all at once, your assignment will lose clarity and appear unstructured. For example, the above assignment task can be broken down into three separate sections:

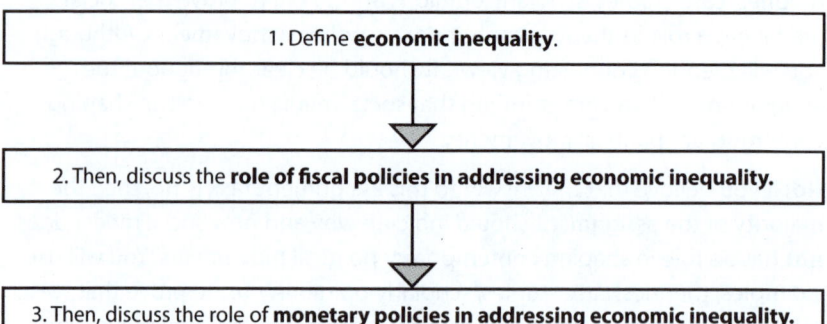

Approach 4: Use AI chatbots and virtual assistants to give you direction

You can use AI chatbots and virtual assistants like ChatGPT, Copilot, etc., to help you respond to assignment tasks. It is important to check with your department's AI guidelines. First, you can use these tools to create an outline for your assignment. For example, you can type in the prompt, 'Can you create an outline for an essay examining gender roles in contemporary British media?' Then, you can expand upon the outline with your own research and original thought. Second, you use them to generate ideas for your assignments. For example, you can input, 'Give me three ideas for my assignment that examines gender roles in contemporary British media.' Then, use what it provides as a starting point for your original research. Third, you can create a title for your project by prompting, 'Can you suggest three titles that would be good for a project on gender roles in contemporary British media?' Then edit the title to suit your preference.

17 How to write an introduction to your assignment

Every assignment should have an introduction. An introduction is the opening paragraph in your assignment; it is the first paragraph that the marker will read, so it needs to be informative and concise. The TAOS (Topic Aim Overview Significance) approach is a simple way to achieve an informative and concise introduction:

1. Topic
2. Aim
3. Overview
4. Significance (optional)

All four of these aspects are enclosed in the first opening paragraph. The general rule is that the introduction should amount to around 10 per cent of your assignment.

1 Topic

The topic is laid out in the first sentences of your introduction; it introduces the audience to the topic words or topic area that your assignment is focused on. For example, if your assignment task is:

> **Evaluate the impact of technological advancements on patient care in the UK.**

Your topic introduction may look like this: *Technological advancements have revolutionized patient care in the United Kingdom, transforming the way healthcare is delivered and experienced.* This is a very effective yet simple introduction to the topic.

Or a more advanced approach is to present the topic as a problem. For example: *It is notoriously difficult to predict how technological advances will interact with patient care.* By problematizing your topic, you can create intrigue and curiosity. You also establish a critical standpoint from the very beginning of your assignment.

You can problematize your topic in several ways:

- You can problematize the topic by indicating that the present situation is unsustainable:
  The shortage of housing, particularly social and genuinely affordable housing, has led to spiralling rents and house prices across the country.

- You can problematize the topic by indicating that matters are worsening:
  Universities are reporting a steep drop in international students applying to come to the UK ...
- You can problematize the topic by indicating that there is a contradiction in the topic:
  Michel Foucault, French historian and philosopher, claimed the question of truth is a question of power. However, there is a performative contradiction in Foucault's account ...

2 Aim

After the topic introduction sentences, you state a clear aim of the assignment. Writing a clear aim is the most important aspect of your introduction. The aim is the foundation; everything rests upon the foundation. Your aim should be a single sentence that describes the intent of your assignment. This sentence should be straightforward and concise. Your aim is derived from the words of the assignment task; you slightly reword or rephrase the assignment task. For example, if your assignment task is: *Assess the impact of urbanization on the health outcomes of children in the UK*, then your rewording can be: *This essay will assess the impact of urbanization on children's health outcomes in the UK*. By starting your rewording with 'This essay will' or 'This report will' or 'This assignment will', you have made your intentions very clear to the marker.

A more advanced approach is to indicate a strong line of argument that will run throughout the assignment. For example, if your assignment task is: *Assess the impact of urbanization on the health outcomes of children in London*, then your rewording can be: *This essay will argue that current levels of urbanization have negatively impacted the health outcomes of children in London*. This rewording makes your position clear; there are no surprises. Even though you will discuss contrasting perspectives, you will demonstrate that the evidence for your position is the weightiest. To give the appearance of balance and impartiality, you need to make sure that you cite as many sources as possible and avoid emotive and informal language.

Another advanced way to reword your aim is to include a particular theory, concept, framework or model. You use a particular theory, concept, framework or model as a lens to look at the assignment topic. A lens provides a structured way to analyse the assignment topic. For example, if your assignment task is: *Assess the impact of urbanization on the health outcomes of children in London*, then your rewording can be: *This essay will utilize Barton's Urban Health model to assess the impact of urbanization on the health outcomes of children in London.* This type of approach demonstrates your creativity and resourcefulness. It is preferable to use a model, theory, concept or framework that was discussed in the module or mentioned in the recommended reading list. It is also important to provide a rationale for using a particular theory, concept, framework or model to look at the topic. For example, your rationale for using Barton's Urban Health model is to provide you with a structured framework of analysis that will help you organize and interpret information, or your rationale for using Barton's Urban Health model is to connect your assignment to the literature; it was common to see Barton's Urban Health model used to look at children's health outcomes. Additionally, when you use a specific theory, concept, framework or model, you do not have to speak about it on every single page of your assignment. However, it must be the dominant approach of your assignment.

The last advanced way to reword your aim is to include a case study. You use a case study as a real-world example of your assignment topic. Essentially, the case study is a typical example of your topic; for example if your topic is the normalization of franchising, you may use McDonald's restaurant as a case study. In this light, the case study can be used to substantiate your central aim. For example, if your assignment task is to *Assess the impact of urbanization on the health outcomes of children in London*, your rewording can be: *This essay will assess the case of Rebecca Simmons to weigh up the impact of urbanization on the health outcomes of children in London.* Once again, this type of approach demonstrates your creativity and resourcefulness. Nonetheless, it is preferable to use a well-documented case study that was discussed in the module or mentioned in the recommended reading. It is also important that you extract general themes from your case study to make sure that you fulfil the assignment task. For example, you extract general themes from the case of Rebecca Simmons that relate to the impact of urbanization on the health outcomes of children in London. Although you will dedicate a section to discuss the specific details of the case of Rebecca Simmons, you will spend much more time extracting general themes from the case of Rebecca Simmons like poor air quality, limited access to natural spaces, dense building areas, etc. Additionally, you will need to provide a rationale for your inclusion of a case study. You will need to explain how your chosen case study enables you to address the assignment task. For example, you can explain that your use of the case of Rebecca Simmons enabled you to explore the intricacies involved in urbanization or demonstrate how abstract theoretical discussions interact in a real-world setting, etc. Refer to page 29 to find case studies.

3 Overview

After you write the aim, you should provide an overview of your entire assignment. The overview is a roadmap in which you briefly describe every major section in your assignment. Your overview should be concise and accurate; from reading your overview, the marker should know exactly what to expect in the order that you mentioned. Here are some examples:

- *This essay will commence with a broad discussion on the definition of populism, including its key features and variations. It will then focus on populism in relation to democratic institutions within the European context. This will be followed by a more detailed discussion on populism's impact on democratic institutions in four critical areas: political parties, electoral systems, policy-making and public discourse.*

- *This essay will cover three areas. The first area will provide a definition of populism, including its key features and variations. Second, there will be a discussion on the impact of populism on European democratic institutions. The third area will explore the resilience and adaptation of European democratic institutions in the face of growing populist movements.*

Writing an overview in the style of above two examples will indicate to the marker that you write in a well-ordered and logical manner. Moreover, writing down the overview will help you structure your assignment; you can use the overview as a roadmap to keep you on track and filter out unnecessary and irrelevant material.

4 Significance (optional)

After the overview, state the significance of your assignment in the last few sentences of the introduction paragraph. The significance needs to be something that is beyond your immediate university experience; you need to explain why your assignment is significant to wider society. Perhaps your lecturer explained the significance of the topic in class, or it was mentioned in the recommended reading list? Here are some possible reasons for the significance of your assignment:

- Your assignment corresponds with a recent government inquiry:
  The assignment's focus on self-driving vehicles is significant because their development and deployment is currently being scrutinized by a government inquiry.

- Your assignment corresponds with an upcoming Act of Parliament:
  This topic is pertinent considering that motorway safety has received increased attention with the enactment of the M48 Motorway Order 2025.

- New statistics have been released:
  This topic is significant due to the release of recent statistics that indicate a substantial population decline in Welsh rural and coastal regions.

Essentially, you are attempting to connect your assignment with what is happening in the real world. This demonstrates to the marker that you are discerning enough to make connections between the assignment task and current affairs. Hear are some example sentences:

- *It is hoped that this assignment will contribute to a deeper understanding of …*
- *Understanding the link between … and … will help …*
- *The importance of this assignment is that it explores …*
- *The assignment should provide some important insights into …*
- *Investigating … is critically important in the understanding of …*
- *This assignment provides an important opportunity to advance our understanding of …*
- *There are several important areas where this assignment makes an important contribution to …*

Example of introduction

Climate change poses risks to companies, financial institutions and individuals alike. Both physical and transition risks could have material impacts on the value of companies and their assets (BEIS, 2022). In this light, this essay will critically evaluate the grounds for making climate-related financial requirements mandatory. This essay will cover four areas. First, there will be a discussion of the material impacts of companies and their assets caused by climate change. Second, this essay will evaluate the theoretical arguments for and against making climate-related financial requirements mandatory. The third area will explore prominent case studies on the issue of climate-related financial

Topic
The topic introduces the audience to the topic.

Aim
The aim is a single, straightforward and concise sentence that describes the intent of your assignment.

Overview
The overview is a roadmap in which you briefly describe every major section in your assignment. Your overview should be concise and accurate.

requirements mandatory. Drawing from the theoretical and practical discussions, the last area will craft an approach to climate-related financial requirements to enhance existing practices and address the growing threat of climate change. Evaluating climate-related financial requirements is deeply significant in the face of mounting opposition and the commitments made by the UK government at the recent United Nations Climate Change Conference.

Significance
State the significance of your assignment in the last few sentences of the introduction paragraph. Explain why your assignment is significant to wider society.

18 How to write the main body of your assignment

The main body of your assignment comprises the paragraphs that come after the introduction. Unlike the introduction, the main body is not titled 'the main body' in your assignment; it is either left blank or named after whatever topic/issue you are discussing.

A good way to write the main body is to use the 'funnel approach'. Mimicking the shape of a funnel, you start broad then gradually narrow your focus to a specific point. Below is an example of the funnel approach. To see what this approach looks like in practice, I will use this approach with an example assignment task: *Assess the impact of populism on European democratic institutions.*

Definition: Define the concepts (topic words) stated in the wording of the assignment task. Be sure to use definitions from academic sources, not dictionaries, lecture notes or your own opinions. Example: The student defines populism, including its key features and variations.

Context: In the previous section, you defined concepts in isolation. Now you need to connect these concepts to the context (restrictive words) stated in the assignment task. Example: the student connects the concept of populism to the context of European democratic institutions. In other words, the student describes the forms of populism found in the European context. The student also begins to develop their critical argument by suggesting that populism has had a problematic relationship within European democratic institutions. If you need to find information on two or more concepts, please refer to a research hack on page 20.

Aim: Focus on the central aim. This should be the largest section – at least 65% of your assignment should be spent carrying out the aim. Example: the student assesses the impact of populism on European democratic institutions. Their critical voice is fully developed in this section; although they show contrasting perspectives, they argue that populism tends to have a negative impact on European democratic institutions.

The way forward: This section seeks to offer a solution or articulate a new vision or reimagination of an issue. This can take the form of pointing to an exemplar that exists in the real-world or theory. Also, it can involve suggesting a model of practice, or model of institution, etc. Up until this point, you have read and cited articles and books, you are now in the best position to make an informed judgement. You have an opportunity to have the last word, which is positive and forward-looking. Example: the student advocates recommendations to enhance the resilience and adaptation of European democratic institutions to address the growing threats of populist movements.

You can merge, add or omit any of the four sections of the funnel approach to suit your specific needs.

The funnel approach example shows four sections; it is important that you write and think about your assignment in clear and distinct sections; avoid free-flowing streams of consciousness. Your marker wants to see a clear structure. You can advertise your structure by explaining in the introduction of your assignment that you have adopted the funnel approach and cite this book:

This assignment will adopt the funnel approach to assess the impact of populism on European democratic institutions (Arthur, 2025). It will start with broad discussion on the definition of populism, including its key features and variations. It will then focus on populism in relation to democratic institutions within the European context. This will be followed by a more detailed discussion on populism's impact on democratic institutions in four critical areas: political parties, electoral systems, policy-making and public discourse.

Additionally, whether you use the funnel approach or not, you should signpost throughout the main body to highlight the structure of your work. Signposting is using phrases and words to guide the reader through the structure of your assignment; it is like holding the reader's hand and guiding them through your assignment. Signposting should be used when you transition from a major section to another major section. Here are some examples:

Scenario	Example words and phrases
Moving from one section to another	*Turning now to …* *Moving on now to consider …* *On the question of …* *Having defined what is meant by … this essay will now move on to discuss …* *With respect to …* *In the case of …* *With regard to …*
Adding to the previous section	*Another significant aspect of … is …* *In addition, it is important to ask …* *Unlike Stringer (2025), Ng (2024) has argued …* *In contrast to Drury (2025), Chatrakul Na Ayudhya (2014) maintains …* *Despite this, little progress has been made in the …* *However, this system also has several serious drawbacks.*

Reminding the reader	*As discussed above, …* *As explained earlier, …* *As previously stated, …* *As indicated previously, …* *As described on the previous page, …* *Returning to the issue of …* *As explained in the introduction, it is clear that …*

19 How to write a conclusion to your assignment

A conclusion is the last section of your assignment. It is the final one or more paragraphs. It is your last opportunity to leave the marker with a favourable impression of your assignment. It is important that you do not include any new information in the conclusion section; you should have covered everything in the main body. A conclusion consists of five aspects. These five aspects are not separated by subheadings. They are contained within one or more paragraphs.

1. **Central conclusion:** You should start the conclusion paragraph by explicitly stating your central conclusion, central message or central point in a single sentence.

   Example: *Through a critical review of the academic literature and government documents, this assignment has demonstrated that the state bears some responsibility in the tragedy of the Grenfell Tower Fire.*

2. **Trail of evidence that led you to your central message:** Briefly summarize the evidential steps that led to the above central point/message/conclusion. What are the key factors? What are the landmark moments? What are the logical steps that you led you to this point?

   Example: *From the trail of evidence from the 1990s, it was possible to conclude that the state had failed the Grenfell residents. This assignment pointed to the state's failure to engage with the research and recommendations from Parliamentary Select Committees coupled with its 'inadequate' and 'poorly operated' pre-Grenfell regulatory system. Both of which created a 'perfect storm' (Davis, 2022, p. 66).*

3. **Broader implications of your central message:** What is the broader lesson that we can learn from your assignment? One broad implication is sufficient. Do not make the broad implication too outlandish or too detached from what you have discussed because you should not add new or unconventional information to a conclusion.

   Example: *The evidence so far points to a grave failure of not just one party, but the entire British state over a prolonged period with devastating consequences. It is an indictment of not just a few politicians but an entire style of government.*

Examples of broad implications:

- Your broad implication could be that you identify the 'real' issue; the 'real' issue that you point to is a root cause or foundational issue that gives rise to other issues. These other issues are secondary to the root cause.

- Your broad implication can be that the future looks bleak: your research has led you to conclude that the future looks bleak because there is no indication of reform or there is a failure to undertake the type of radical action needed. There is no planned legislation or government enquiry; there is nothing on the horizon.

- Your broad implication may be that your research has led you to believe that the future looks promising; perhaps you have observed the setting up of government committees, planned legislation or increased awareness.

- Your broad implication is that an issue has been underestimated. Your research has revealed that the real extent of this issue is largely unknown or maybe the focus is on one particular aspect, whereas you have identified a more problematic aspect that has not been widely discussed.

- Your broad implication is that your research revealed that the problem or issue has been overstated or amplified; there are more troubling matters that we need focus on.

- Your broad implication is that the focus should be on the system or the environment not the individual. Your research revealed that even though individuals have been labelled or stigmatized, the real issue is systemic.

- Your broad implication can be that the issue is a growing ethical dilemma. Your research reveals a crossroads; in order to progress, an ethical choice has to be made. As a society, we must choose one of the paths.

4. **Future directions** (optional): Indicate areas where further research is needed. Perhaps you struggled to find information on a particular area, or you discovered a new development that hasn't yet been accounted for in the literature. Indicating areas where further research is needed shows that you have a deep understanding of the topic and can think critically about its broader context.

   Example: *The literature was sparse on the susceptibility of the state to the well-managed campaigns of lobbyists from the cladding industry. It would be interesting to know more about the level of reliance that the state had on the information from the cladding industry and why this was the case.*

5. **Final thought:** End with a strong and impactful statement.

    Example: *Moving forward, it is imperative that these lessons lead to tangible changes in how we design, manage and inhabit our urban environments. By doing so, we honour the memory of those lost and ensure that such a tragedy is never repeated.*

    This final sentence can either be:

    - A call to action: *Moving forward, it is vital that senior leadership and academics work together to create inclusive classrooms where all students can thrive.*

    - Or a thought-provoking question: *Given the overwhelming benefits of renewable energy, the question remains: How long can society afford to delay its widespread implementation?*

    - Or a vision for the future: *Envisioning a future shaped by a multi-party system that is truly representative of the British electorate is all the motivation needed to pursue electoral reform.*

    - Or a quote: *'Not everything that is faced can be changed, but nothing can be changed until it is faced.'*

    - Or a challenge to the reader: *The evidence is clear, and the steps have been laid out. The challenge now lies in the academic community's willingness to embrace the transformative potential of AI pedagogies.*

Part 4

How to build arguments

How to build an argument

At all levels of university study, you will be expected to use arguments to convey information. An argument is a point of view that is supported by evidence. Evidence is information that you extract from journal articles, reports or academic books. An argument without evidence is just an opinion. For example:

Tottenham Football Club is the wealthiest sports club in London.

The above statement is just an opinion because it is not supported by evidence. However, if you substantiate this opinion with data from reports, articles or books to support this statement, it now becomes an argument; as follows:

Tottenham Football Club is the wealthiest sports club in London. Johnson (2024) explains that this is due to the development of Tottenham's new stadium, which has significantly increased revenue for football and non-football events.

What is building an argument?

Essentially, building an argument is writing down the evidence you have gathered from journal articles, reports or academic books to put forward a point of view. This is a difficult process because it requires you to integrate various sources of evidence to make a coherent point. It is akin to a baker who mixes various ingredients to make a cake or an artist who uses a variety of colours to produce a painting.

What weakens an argument?

In most cases, an argument is weakened by three matters:

1. It is weakened by writing in the first person (I, me, you, we) because it gives the impression that the argument is impartial. Instead, you are generally expected to write in the third person; for example, instead of writing 'I will use Johnson's definition', you should write, 'This essay will use Johnson's definition'.

2. An argument is also weakened by using emotive and colloquial language, such as, 'This is horrifying', 'This is ridiculous', or 'This is the pot calling the kettle black' because it can be perceived as too informal or too impartial.

3. It is difficult for the marker to see how the evidence you extracted from journal articles, reports or academic books relates to your claim. Therefore, whenever you make a claim, make sure that your evidence is explicitly and directly related to your claim.

This Part will present six argument templates:

20. Basic argument
21. The however factor
22. There can only be one
23. The magic number
24. The middle ground
25. The real world

Each template is colour-coded, fully described and assigned an example to ease understanding and implementation. These templates will help you structure your writing. Structure is vital to the clarity and acceptability of an argument. A well-structured argument indicates to the person marking your work that you have fully developed critical thinking, research and communication skills.

20 Basic argument

The first template is titled 'the basic argument'. This template is an effective way to put forward a point of view that is supported by evidence. By using this template, you can demonstrate to the marker that you are able to present your research and ideas in a coherent and systematic way.

When should you use this template?

This is a common template that is primarily used in the main body of an assignment to put forward a point of view that is supported by evidence.

Description

A basic argument structure comprises three parts. These three parts come together to form one paragraph:

1. **The introduction sentence** is the opening sentence that puts forward a clear and explicit point of view or a claim. It also gives an overview of the argument. It is vital to give an introduction sentence before jumping straight to the evidence, so the reader is aware of your intent.

2. **Evidence sentences** follow the introduction sentence. Evidence sentences are quotes or paraphrases from books, articles or reports that substantiate the claim of the introduction sentence. This part is crucial because it supports the claim you made in the introduction sentence. Without these evidence sentences, the introduction sentence is just an opinion. Moreover, writing evidence sentences demonstrates to the marker that you have researched the topic.

3. **The verdict sentence** is the closing sentence where you give a statement or verdict about the evidence sentences. The 'verdict should follow the evidence'. Also, the verdict sentence concludes the argument – whenever you produce an argument, you should clarify where you stand. As in most cases of academic writing, this sentence should be written in the third person and should not include emotive or colloquial language.

Example of basic argument

Canada's publicly funded healthcare system is among the best in the world. Smith (2025) explains that the Canadian system ensures equal healthcare access through social assistance. Moreover, Cann (2024) states that Canada's healthcare system prioritizes primary care services over specialist consultations. For these reasons, the healthcare system represents an exemplar of publicly funded healthcare.

> This **introduction sentence** puts forward a claim and also informs the reader about the topic of the entire paragraph.

> These **evidence sentences** support the claim in the introduction sentence. These evidence sentences are crucial to gaining high marks; the more evidence you can show in your writing, the higher your grades will be.

> After you provide the evidence sentences, you write a **verdict sentence** because the 'verdict follows the evidence'.

As you can see from the above example, the introduction sentence informs the reader about the subject of the entire argument. Furthermore, try to start all paragraphs with an introduction sentence, even if you are not putting forward an argument. This will make your writing easier to follow. If you start a paragraph or argument without an introduction sentence, it may be difficult for the reader to keep track. Additionally, it will be difficult to decipher what purpose your evidence serves, for example:

> Johnson (2025) found that three out of four UK companies pay their male staff more than their female staff.

> This is evidence, but because there is no introduction sentence, it is too difficult to decipher what purpose your evidence serves. We have no idea of the intent of the writer.

> Despite significant advances in legislation and policy, there is widespread evidence that men continue to earn more than their female counterparts. Johnson (2023) found that three out of four UK companies pay their male staff more than their female staff.

> By adding an introduction sentence, it is clear why the evidence is being used.

21 The however factor

The second template is titled 'the however factor'. This template is an effective way to present two contrasting perspectives on a single issue. By using this template, you can demonstrate to the marker that you are able to gather and articulate two different perspectives.

When should you use the however factor?

This is a common template that is primarily used in the main body of an assignment to show a diversity of scholarly opinions.

Description

The 'however factor' structure comprises five parts. These five parts come together to form one or more paragraphs:

1. Write the introduction sentence, which is the opening sentence that asserts that there are contrasting perspectives on a specific issue. It is vital to make this clear before jumping straight to the differing perspectives, so the reader is aware of your intent.

    Example introduction sentences:

    - *Scholars have long debated the …*
    - *There has been much disagreement between scholars on the subject of …*
    - *There has been disagreement on the criteria for defining …*
    - *One of the most significant current discussions in … is between …*
    - *To date there has been little agreement on …*
    - *A much-debated question is whether …*
    - *Debate has long prevailed as to whether …*
    - *The relationship between … and … has attracted conflicting interpretations from …*
    - *Several contrasting accounts of … have been proposed, creating numerous controversies.*
    - *The causes of … have been the subject of intense debate …*
    - *In the literature on … the relative importance of … has been subject to considerable discussion.*

2. Then write the first perspective of a scholar. Try to give a concise and fair account of this perspective. Imagine the person reading your work is ignorant of this perspective.
3. Then add 'however' after the first perspective to signal that you are about to introduce a contrasting perspective. You do not need to use the word 'however'; you can use 'alternatively', 'in contrast', 'contrastingly', 'on the other hand', etc.
4. Then write the contrasting perspective, derived from the work of another scholar. Try to give a concise and fair account of this perspective. Imagine the person reading your work is ignorant of this perspective.

    Example sentences:

    - *Mohamed (2025) disputes this account of …*
    - *Ellermeier (2024) challenges the widely held view that …*
    - *However, Jones (2024) points out that …*
    - *The idea that … was first challenged by Lee (2004).*
    - *Alghamdi (2024) is critical of the tendency to …*
    - *However, Jewitt (2020) questioned this premise and …*
    - *Ribeiro (2016) has challenged some of Pinder's conclusions, arguing that …*
    - *Another major criticism of Smith's study made by Adeyeye (2025) is that …*
    - *In her discussion of … Wilson-Thain (2026) criticizes the ways in which some authors …*
    - *Huda's rejection of Huxley's explanation merits some discussion …*
    - *In a recent article, Smith (2026) questions the extent to which …*
    - *The latter point has been critiqued by Xu (2026), who argues that …*
    - *A recently published article by Clement (2025) casts doubts on Jones's assumption that …*
    - *Other authors (see Charles, 2026; Lee, 2025) question the usefulness of such an approach …*

5. Then provide a verdict on the two scholarly perspectives; in other words, state which perspective is the most valid and explain why. A scholarly perspective may be more valid than another because it is more up to date, provides weightier evidence, has scholarly consensus, is more specific, is more comprehensive, has better methodology, etc.

Examples of evaluative adjectives to describe your selected perspective	Verdict sentences to describe why you selected a particular perspective
timely seminal detailed thorough excellent influential important innovative pioneering impressive wide-ranging comprehensive groundbreaking	• *The most comprehensive study of … during this period has been undertaken by* • *Kent's study remains one of the most comprehensive studies of* • *Lamar's 2021 study is particularly helpful* • *One of the most influential accounts comes from Kettle* • *Kray's research is valuable for an understanding of* • *Monet's account of … provides us with a useful lens through which* • *A more detailed analysis of the longer-term impact of … can be found in Arturo's recent article in* • *The pioneering work of Kay and John remains crucial to our wider understanding of*

Example of the however factor

The introduction of AI into the educator's toolbox has been the subject of intense debate. On one hand, Karim and Baker (2025) argue that interactive AI tools, such as virtual tutors and chatbots, can impart knowledge and engage students in new and innovative ways, making learning more interactive and enjoyable. However, on the other hand, Jewitt (2020) questioned this premise. She argued that education is not just about imparting knowledge; it's also about mentoring and human interaction. Over-reliance on AI can reduce the personal connection between educators and students, potentially impacting the quality of education and student well-being.

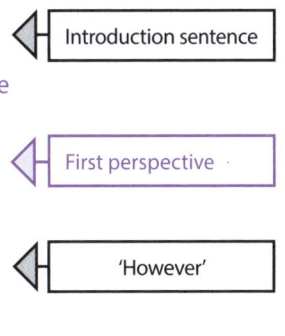

Though both perspectives have merit, Karim's study (2020) is rooted in the current context of the massification of higher education in which students significantly outnumber lecturers. In an ideal situation, Jewitt's argument is undeniable, but in the current climate, interactive AI tools used prudently, offer a viable alternative.

The verdict sentence in this example is the most critical part of the paragraph. By selecting Karim, you are showing discernment and critical judgement. When you write this verdict sentence(s), write it in third person and avoid emotive and colloquial language.

> This example is a summarized paragraph; your use of this template may amount to two paragraphs or even a whole page.

22 There can only be one

This template is titled 'there can only be one'. It is an effective way to present several definitions or interpretations and then select one and explain why you selected it. This will demonstrate to the marker that you have read widely and have heightened levels of critical discernment.

When should you use 'there can only be one'?

This template can be used at the beginning of your assignment to present several definitions and then select the best definition to use for the rest of the assignment. In most assignments, you should define the main term(s) in your assignment question. This is because, in most disciplines, one term may carry several definitions or interpretations. For example, the term 'community' has been defined in numerous ways over the past few decades. This is because scholars who defined the term 'community' have come from differing intellectual traditions or different places in the world or have written at different times. Therefore, if the term 'community' is part of your assignment question, it would be prudent to state what you mean by 'community'.

You can also use this template generally, not just for definitions, but also to present a variety of scholarly perspectives on a specific occurrence or differing scholarly verdicts on the validity of an approach, etc. Whenever you want to show that there is more than one understanding, this template is for you.

Description

This argument template comprises three parts. These three parts come together to form one paragraph:

1. **Write the introduction sentence,** which is the opening sentence that asserts that there are contrasting perspectives on a specific issue. It is vital to make this clear before jumping straight to the differing perspectives, so the reader is aware of your intent.

    Example sentences:
    - *The definition of ... has evolved.*
    - *There are multiple definitions of ...*

- *Several definitions of … have been proposed.*
- *The term … embodies several concepts which …*
- *This term has two overlapping meanings. First, …*
- *Despite its common usage, … is used in different disciplines to mean different things.*
- *Since the definition of … varies among scholars, it is important to clarify how the term is used in …*

2. **The evidence sentences** present a variety of definitions or interpretations that are found in journal articles, books or reports.

3. **The verdict sentence** is where you choose which definition, interpretation or scholarly opinion is the most appropriate and explain why you believe it is the most appropriate. You may have chosen it because you believe that it is the most comprehensive; most specific; most up to date; in line with the majority position; most widespread and accepted definition; incorporates race, gender, class, age or neurodiversity; offered the most clarity, etc. Write this verdict sentence(s) in third person and avoid emotive and colloquial language.

Example of 'there can only be one'

Human capital has acquired several definitions over the decades. Schultz (1961) proposed that human capital consists of knowledge, skills and abilities of the people employed in an organization. Bontis (1999) defines human capital as the human factor that gives the organization its distinctive character. Thomas (2013) describes human capital as the performance and potential of people within the organization. This essay will utilize Thomas's work due to its inclusion of the term 'potential', which suggests that organizations can use people to develop over time.

 This introduction sentence states that there are a variety of definitions for 'human capital'.

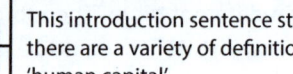 These evidence sentences present three definitions of 'human capital'.

 This verdict sentence is the most critical part of the paragraph. If you merely provide a summary of various definitions, this may come across as being too passive. However, by selecting Thomas's definition and justifying the selection, you are showing discernment and critical judgement. When you write this verdict sentence(s), write it in third person and avoid emotive and colloquial language.

23 The middle ground

This template is titled 'the middle ground' argument. It is the most evolved form of argumentation. It presents two contrasting perspectives, then seeks to find middle ground between both perspectives. This approach is rooted in reconciliation rather than dispute and to defuse rather than to ignite.

When should you use the middle ground?

This template should be used if you come across two seemingly contrasting perspectives, but you are able to find some way to bridge these perspectives. Though there are differences, you can see a commonality between perspectives, even if it is very slight.

Description

This argument template comprises three parts. These three parts come together to form one or more paragraphs:

1. Write the introduction sentence, which is the opening sentence that asserts that there are contrasting perspectives on a specific issue.
2. The evidence sentences describe the source of disagreement between two perspectives. You play the role of a narrator describing their differences.

   Example sentences:
   - *There is a notable disagreement between Johnson and Williams regarding …*
   - *While Anderson asserts that …, Brown contends that …*
   - *The primary point of contention between Richards and Kim is …*
   - *At the heart of their debate is the question of whether …*

3. Then write a verdict sentence(s) that proposes a way to unite these two differing perspectives. This can take many forms; you can argue that the similarities between the two perspectives outweigh their differences. Therefore, the disagreement is largely cosmetic and should be brushed aside.

   Example sentences:
   - *Both … and … share several key features.*
   - *There are several similarities between … and*
   - *Both … and … are concerned with*
   - *Both …and … were developed for similar purposes.*

Additionally, you can argue that it is possible to amalgamate between the perspectives to create a hybrid perspective. For example: *Though Johnson and Andrews adopt divergent approaches, they in fact complement each other in their centring of culture; in this area, it is possible to craft an approach that incorporates both of their works. This approach would utilize Johnson's notion of memory alongside Andrews's concept of nostalgia.*

Also, you can argue that one party has misinterpreted the other, therein creating disagreement, so you clear up this confusion in an effort to bring both parties together. For example: *King's repudiation of Mills's concept of agency is due to King's limited reading of Mills. It is correct that Mills (1999) gives a restrictive definition of agency. However, Mills's (2005, 2009) later work expands on this definition and incorporates structure; Mills explicitly states that women and other marginalized groups navigate and resist oppressive structures, thereby asserting their agency within and against these constraints. Considering Mills's later development, it is clear that there is significant agreement between Mills and King.*

Example of the middle ground

There is a notable difference between Shakur and Wallace regarding the role of technology in higher education. — Introduction sentence

Their difference appears to stem from the importance given to technology; Shakur gives it prime importance. He sees technology as a way to bridge educational gaps and prepare students for a technologically advanced future. However, Wallace argues that an overemphasis on digital tools can undermine fundamental skills such as critical thinking, problem-solving and face-to-face communication. — Description of the disagreement between two perspectives.

Despite their contrasting perspectives on the role of technology in education, both Wallace and Shakur find common ground in the emphasis on student engagement. They both agree that the goal of any educational strategy should be to engage students actively and meaningfully. This shared emphasis on engagement underscores the importance of considering how various tools can best serve students' needs, highlighting that while their approaches differ, their objectives align in fostering a dynamic and effective learning environment. — Verdict sentence that seeks to find a middle ground between both perspectives. When you write this verdict sentence(s), write it in third person and avoid emotive and colloquial language.

24 The real world

This template is titled 'the real-world argument'. It incorporates a real-world example into your argument in order to substantiate your conceptual idea. For example, you may discuss 'creative destruction', which is a concept that describes a process in which new innovations replace older innovations. This concept may be too difficult to grasp, so you make it 'real' by connecting creative destruction with the real-world example of how Netflix and streaming services gradually replaced Blockbuster and video rental stores.

When should you use the real-world argument?

This template serves three needs. First, incorporating real-world information into your argument can be used to substantiate a claim. For example, you may claim in your assignment that specific steps are needed to reach corporate sustainability, so you provide a real-world example of Nike's steps to attain corporate sustainability that were identical to the steps that you outlined. Second, real-world information can be used to evidence what is likely to happen if your recommendations are not heeded. For example, you use a real-world example of McDonald's decline in productivity to indicate the possible consequence of fast-food restaurants that do not increase their range of healthier options. Third, you may need to distinguish between two concepts, so you provide real-world examples to make the distinction clear. For example, you may need to distinguish individual racism from institutional racism, so you present a real-world example of each.

Description

This argument template comprises three parts. These three parts come together to form one or more paragraphs:

1. Write the introduction sentence, which is the opening sentence that puts forward a claim, statement or explanation. Your claim, statement or explanation may extend beyond a sentence.
2. Add connecting words or phrases to connect the above claim, statement or explanation with your real-world example.

    Example sentences:

    - *An example of this is …*
    - *To give a well-known example …*

- *This is exemplified by …*
- *This distinction is exemplified in …*
- *The effectiveness of … has been exemplified by …*
- *The ineffectiveness of … has been exemplified by …*
- *This is evident in the case of …*
- *This is certainly true in the case of …*
- *The evidence of … can be clearly seen in the case of …*
- *In a similar case …*
- *This can be seen in the case of …*
- *… is a good illustration of …*
- *… illustrates this point clearly.*
- *This can be illustrated briefly by …*
- *The most striking illustration of this is …*
- *By way of illustration …*

3. Describe the real-world example: this example must be a specific development, occurrence, activity, event, consequence or process that happened or is happening in the real world, which we can draw conclusions and learn from. This example needs to be documented; you need to be able to cite it from books, articles, reports or websites from reputable organizations. It cannot be something that you personally experienced or observed, unless you are writing a reflection. Please refer to page 29 for a hack to find real-world information.

4. Then write a verdict sentence that reiterates what the reader should understand from your real-world example; what is the key take-away from the real world? How does the real-world example help us understand your claim, statement or explanation.

   Examples:
   - *This case has shown that …*
   - *The case reported here illustrates the …*
   - *From this example, it is evident that …*
   - *Overall, this case supports the view that …*
   - *This example confirms the importance of …*
   - *It is evident from the example given here that …*
   - *The evidence presented thus far supports the idea that …*
   - *This case demonstrates the need for better strategies for …*
   - *As this case demonstrates, it is important that …*

Example of the real-world argument

Climate change is often associated with the destructive influence of excess heat and flooding but less so with the insidious erosion of health by the indoor 'breathed environment' (Smith, 2023, p. 5). The most striking illustration of this is Awaab Ishak died in a small apartment in Rochdale, Greater Manchester, on 21 December 2020, shortly after his second birthday. The autopsy found that Awaab's airways were swollen to a degree that would compromise his breathing, and fungus was detected in his blood and lungs along with evidence of severe allergic granulomatous inflammation (Holgate, 2024). This case has shown that beyond the headlines, climate change is impacting the quality of individual lives; the mould spores that were present in Awaab's small apartment are ubiquitous and will only take hold if the temperature and humidity are suitable. Climate change is a key factor in creating these conditions of condensation and dampness in housing.

Introduction sentence: Making a statement about climate change.

Connecting climate change to the real-world example of Awaab Ishak.

Description of the real-world example of Awaab Ishak.

Then the verdict sentence reiterates the central reason of presenting the Awaab Ishak case.

25 The magic number

This template brings all your related points into a numerical list. By bringing together your related points, you enhance your overall argument. This is because weaker arguments, packed together, are strengthened; just as individual weaker fingers are strengthened by forming a fist. Additionally, this template enhances the coherence and structure of your writing.

When should you use the magic number argument?

This template can be used in two occasions. First, you seek to be persuasive; you intend to articulate several points to prove or disprove. Instead of arguing separate points, bring them under one umbrella to make your points more cohesive. Second, you can use this template in your general academic writing; it does not have to be an argument, you can use it to make the reader aware of several related matters, factors, causes, issues or situations.

Description

This argument template comprises three parts. These three parts come together to form one or more paragraphs:

1. Write the introduction sentence that gives the reader an overview of your list.

   Example sentences:
   - *The three key aspects of management can be listed as follows:*
   - *There are two basic approaches to …*
   - *There are two types of effect which result when …*
   - *There are three reasons why …*
   - *There are several possible reasons for the lack of literature:*
   - *The disadvantages of … stem from three matters*
   - *The advantages of … are rooted in four matters*

   Alternatively, you can write an introduction sentence that gives the reader an overview of other people's lists.

Example sentences:

- *Lu and Xu (2025) highlight three major causes of failure.*
- *Adebayor (2023) lists the main features of …*
- *Henry (2022) argues that there are two broad categories of …*
- *Palmer (2020) suggests three conditions for …*
- *For Baldwin, discrimination is of four kinds …*

2. List the matters in numerical order (First, then discuss the first matter. Second, then the discuss the second matter. Third, then discuss the third matter, etc.). Each matter can be discussed in one paragraph or, if there is a lot of information, you can start a new paragraph to discuss the second matter, then start a new paragraph to discuss the third matter, etc. Whether your list is contained within one paragraph or several paragraphs, try not to list beyond five; it can get tedious and difficult to follow.

3. Write a verdict sentence that explains the central reason that you brought all these points together. What do you want the reader to gather from all these points?

Examples:

- *These factors have shown that …*
- *The issues outlined here illustrate the …*
- *From these studies, it is evident that …*
- *Overall, these studies support the view that …*
- *These points confirm the importance of …*
- *The evidence presented thus far supports the idea that …*

Example of the magic number

For several reasons, it is futile for universities to rely on the development of AI detection tools to detect the use of AI in student work. First, AI has attracted considerable funding to the extent that AI detection services cannot compete with the vast resources of Microsoft, Open AI and Google (Furze, 2024). Second, students can use prompting tactics that are designed to circumvent detection tools (Smith, 2025). Third, false positives are risks that most university departments

> Introduction sentence alerts the reader that there are several items to discuss.

> The reasons why reliance on AI detection is futile are listed in numerical order.

are not willing to take (Lucas, 2025). <u>Fourth</u>, the additional workload that AI detection tools demand is beyond what most departments can bear (Kay, 2026). Unlike plagiarism tools, using large language models does not give a clearcut result. Therefore, staff will need to spend much more time investigating and administering the extra paperwork from appeals (Simpson, 2024). **These reasons should hinder efforts to rely solely on AI detection tools. It may be possible to overcome one of these hurdles but not all four.**

> The verdict sentences explain why you listed the difficulties of relying on AI detection tools.

Example of not using the magic number

AI has attracted considerable funding to the extent that AI detection services cannot compete with the vast resources of Microsoft, Open AI and Google. Students can use prompting tactics that are designed to circumvent detection tools. False positives are risks that most university departments are not willing to take. Litigation is commonplace in most universities. The additional workload that AI detection tools demand is beyond what most departments can bear. Unlike plagiarism tools, using large language models does not give a clearcut result. Therefore, staff will need to spend much more time investigating and administering the extra paperwork from appeals.

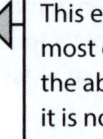

> This example contains most of the wording of the above example, but it is not using the magic number template. Without the template, this example seems more disorganized and harder to follow.

Part 5

How to critique academic texts

How to critique academic texts

This section will give you practical techniques to criticize academic texts *directly*. Imagine that you are reading an academic text, and you want to find ways to criticize the text directly without having to refer to the work of other scholars. You may not have the knowledge or confidence to do it yourself, therefore, this Part will provide you with six approaches to criticize texts with full confidence.

26. Critiquing academic texts using the 'generic' approach

27. Critiquing academic texts using the 'limitations' approach

28. Critiquing academic texts using the 'new' approach

29. Critiquing academic texts using the 'outdated' approach

30. Critiquing academic texts using the 'race, gender or class' approach

Criticizing scholarship is crucial to improving your grades and enhancing the quality of your academic work. Thus, these five techniques have been made malleable and adaptable to your specific academic writing needs.

26 Critiquing academic texts using the 'generic' approach

If you find an academic text in the same topic area as your assignment, but it has a broader scope than your assignment, you can criticize the text. From the text's title or abstract, you can ascertain if it has a broader scope than your assignment. A broader scope is having a broader geographical range than your assignment or it covers a wider time period, larger population sample, etc. This leaves the text open to your criticism. For example, if your assignment is focused on early childhood interventions in the UK, you can critique a text that focuses on early childhood interventions in Europe. Your argument is that the text is too generic, too broad or too non-specific to use for your assignment. Europe is a large geographical area, whereas your assignment is a more focused, nuanced and concentrated study of the UK. Likewise, if your assignment topic is focused on a specific population group's susceptibility to climate change, you can critique a text which looks at the whole population's susceptibility to climate change. If your assignment topic is focused on an event that occurred in a particular time period, you can critique a text that looks at the same event, but over a broader time period. For example:

- *Jutley's study is <u>too broad</u> to contribute to this discussion.*
- *His study is <u>too generic</u> to contribute to this focused investigation.*
- *The research provides sweeping coverage of … that neglects to address the nuanced factors that this assignment is concerned with.*

Strengthening the generic approach

Although criticizing a text for being too broad is a good start, it is not enough. You need to extend this criticism. This can be done in four ways. You can apply these four ways independently or merge them:

1. **Selectivity:** In your criticism, you acknowledge that there is some value in a text. However, taken as a whole, you argue that the text's broad coverage is not beneficial to your focused investigation. Generally, if you find a text in a similar topic area as your assignment, it will contain some valuable information. Acknowledgement of some value is a demonstration of critical analysis because it shows selectivity; you take an aspect and leave other aspects, or you can see value in a particular

section, but when you zoom out and you see the entire text, its value decreases to the extent that it is not useful to your assignment.

Examples:

- *Lucas's synthesis of the two models is innovative, but the broadness of their application overlooks crucial contextual details.*
- *While the study offers a broad overview, it lacks the detailed examination necessary to benefit.*
- *Although there is some value in Lee's discussion on the nature of factory legislation, his broad sweep of the nineteenth century takes away from its nuanced and incremental development.*

2. **Problematization:** Build on your criticism of broadness by explaining why generality is a problem. Just because something is general, it does not necessarily mean that it is a problem. Thus, you need to articulate the reasons why the text's generic approach is a problem. It may be a problem because a wide-ranging approach obfuscates and blurs crucial details; in doing so, we are not able to get an accurate or full picture of the plight of some groups, sectors, industries, governments, etc. Therein, the generic text's neglect of specific concerns becomes your main point of contention with the text. Correspondingly, it may be a problem because covering too many areas leads to a superficial treatment of the topic. This results in a lack of depth in the analysis and a failure to provide thorough insights.

Examples:

- *Lewis fails to appreciate the importance of focusing on a single industry. Her broad approach does not reveal the unique challenges and opportunities faced by individual industries.*
- *His conflation of communities prevents us from seeing an accurate picture of each community. Therefore, his work does not go far enough to explore the nuances of the data collected.*
- *He has not taken into account recent studies that focus on smaller units (Lee, 2025; King, 2026). These studies have provided us with considerably more insight into the development of Sub-Saharan African tech startups.*

3. **Categorization:** You can categorize studies into groups. Categorization is a critical activity; it resembles the original meaning of 'critic', which is 'to separate, to sieve, to decide, to distinguish'. Categorization demonstrates to the marker that you have the expertise to provide an overview of the literature. It shows that you can take a step back and review the entire literature field, not just individual studies. The example

below categorizes broad studies and evidences the categorization with citations.

Example:

- *There are several studies that take a broad international approach (Pitt, 2023; Lee, 2020; Kettle, 2022).*

Moreover, you can contrast the more general studies with the more specific studies. Example:

- *There are several studies that explore the impact of artificial intelligence (AI) across sectors (Jones, 2025; Walters, 2023; John, 2022; Luther, 2022). In contrast some scholars have taken a different approach by focusing on AI's impact on specific sectors, such as healthcare, agriculture and education (Jones, 2025; Walters, 2023; John, 2022; Luther, 2022). This latter strand provides us with a more nuanced understanding of how AI use interacts with established systems and these studies were able to provide more specific and actionable recommendations than their broader counterparts.*

Categorization should become part of your research process. As shown in the example below, just jot down studies that take a broad approach and studies that adopt a more specific approach, then incorporate this into your writing. You can even go beyond the simple general vs specific; you can categorize whatever is relevant to your assignment; pre-legislation vs post-legislation, primary research vs secondary research, pre-Covid-19 vs post-Covid-19, UK vs US, etc.

UK-focused studies	International studies
John, 2024 Green, 2021 Samson, 2025	Henry, 2022 Lin, 2020 Otis, 2024

4. **Suggestion:** Build on your criticism of broadness by suggesting that the author of the text adopts a specific approach. The suggestions must be specific, constructive and respectful. This form of critique demonstrates your maturity and discernment.

   Examples:

   - *A further study with more focus on … is therefore suggested.*
   - *Due to the broadness of the author's research topic, several questions remain unanswered. It would have been informative to know how*

the application of the model would have performed in specific boroughs.

- *Further work is required to establish the viability of the framework in specific industries.*
- *These results warrant further investigation with a more specific study on …*
- *Another potentially fruitful avenue for future research is to apply this concept in less diverse settings.*

Use the four approaches (selectivity, problematization, categorization and suggestion) independently or merge them to enhance your critique of generic texts.

If we can critique texts that are too generic, then can we also critique texts that are too specific?

Yes, if you come across a text that takes a more detailed and specific approach, you can critique it. There are several lines of argument that you can use:

- You can argue that the text has limited value because it does not 'zoom out' to get a better picture of what is happening across the entire industry/sector/population, etc.
- You can argue that the text neglects broader implications.
- You can argue that the text's specificity results in a limited contribution to the knowledge because it can be challenging to integrate highly specific findings into the broader literature field.
- You can argue that the text does not consider broader contexts or related factors that could influence the issue being studied.
- You can argue that policymakers and practitioners might find it difficult to apply the findings of very specialized studies.

27 Critiquing academic texts using the 'limitations' approach

If a text states its limitations, you can use those same limitations to critique it. Essentially, we can turn their limitations into our criticism. Limitations are the author's acknowledgement of the weaknesses or constraints of their study. Authors reveal the limitations of their research to foster transparency, future research and critical evaluation.

Step-by-step guide to criticizing a text using its limitations

1. **Find limitations:** Most journal articles will state their limitations. Generally, this can be found towards the end of the article or occasionally articles will have a section titled 'limitations'. There is no set rule for where the limitations should be, so if the limitations are not found in the places mentioned, then scan through the whole article to find where the author revealed the limitations of their article.

2. **Paraphrase the limitations:** Once you have found the limitations, paraphrase them into your own words. For example, imagine that you see this sentence below in a journal article:

   > A limitation of my research is that there is no detailed discussion of the complex web of relationships that exists between branch managers.

   You paraphrase the above sentence to become:

   > The article fails to detail the intricate web of relationships that typifies decision-making contexts.
   >
   > Or
   >
   > The article offers a simplistic account of the complex web of relationships.

3. **Extend the limitation:** Your paraphrase of the limitation is not enough. The author believes that limitation does not affect the study. Therefore, you need to elaborate on your critique of the limitation. You need to explain why this limitation is not acceptable. For example:

> The study's failure to detail the intricate web of relationships is problematic for two reasons. First, by not detailing the intricate relationships, the author opted for oversimplification. This can lead to a superficial understanding of the networks of branch managers. Second, complex relationships often include subtleties and nuances that are critical for a full comprehension of the networks of branch managers.

4. **Situate your dissertation/assignment (optional):** You can use the limitations of a text to position your dissertation/assignment as a 'redeemer'. Your dissertation/assignment will address the limitations; it has come to 'right the wrongs' of the text. This line of argument provides your dissertation/assignment with a greater significance; your dissertation/assignment builds on what was before to enhance the topic area. For example:

    - *This dissertation aims to address Pedley's limitations in two ways …*
    - *This section will fill the gaps left by Sinfield's failure to detail the complex web of relationships.*
    - *The dissertation is situated in the gaps highlighted by Burn's study of branch managers.*
    - *By using in-person interviews, this research will amend Simon's methodological approach.*

28 Critiquing academic texts using the 'new' approach

This form of critique confronts all that is professed to be new. Most matters develop incrementally, rarely do we experience dramatic change abruptly. Moreover, there is always something in the 'new' that has similarities with the 'old'.

The criticism against the 'new' usually takes two forms:

1 The text states that something has changed

This text states that something has changed; this change may be a new infrastructure, new attitudes, new challenges, etc. The reason for stating that something has changed is usually due to the text's need to justify its new approach. If nothing has changed, there is very little need for its new approach, so the author goes to great lengths to explain that something has changed.

Our response to their assumption of change is that not much has changed, change has been minimal or it's too difficult to see where the change occurred. Moreover, you can allege that the author has exaggerated the change; you can evidence the author's exaggeration by pointing to constants or similarities with the past.
Examples:

- *The author fails to provide sufficient evidence of why post-Covid-19 working from home arrangements differ dramatically from pre-Covid-19 arrangements.*

- *The text lacks a thorough examination of the historical context, which is essential to understand whether the reported change is as significant as the author assumes.*

- *While the study reports a significant change, there are at least three significant similarities with previous committee reports.*

- *Although the study highlights a change, it does not go into enough detail about the extent of this change, leaving readers with an incomplete understanding of what exactly has changed.*

- *His discussion on the recent rise in conspiracy theories does not consider that the digital space merely offers a new form of expression for significantly older far-right conspiracies.*

2 The text states it is bringing a new approach

This text's new approach can be in the form of a new theory, framework, concept, model, pedagogy, etc. This new thing that is being brought forward is heralded as an update to something that is defunct or outdated. Alternatively, it may be an amalgamation of two or more older theories, frameworks, concepts, models, pedagogies, etc.

Our response to this new approach is that it is not entirely new, or we have existing approaches that do similar things. Also, it is difficult to see if the new approach will take us somewhere new. We are essentially classifying these new approaches as 'old wines in new bottles'. To compare and contrast existing approaches with the new approach, refer to where the author references previous works; most new approaches will mention previous works in an effort to show the sources and inspiration of their new approach. Once you find the previous works, compare and contrast with the new approach.
Examples:

- *King's model (2004) is not particularly new, he merely adds a few contextual details to Crites's older model (1988) of vocational adjustment.*
- *The novelty claimed by the author is minimal and does not represent a significant departure from Freire's foundational idea.*
- *It is not entirely clear why Siemens and Downes developed (2008) their connectivity approach because there are several existing approaches that can be harnessed for digital education.*
- *The author fails to adequately explain how her new approach improves upon or addresses the limitations of the existing approaches, making it difficult to justify its necessity.*
- *The similarities between the author's framework and existing frameworks raise questions about the originality and added value of her study.*

29 Critiquing academic texts using the 'outdated' approach

If a text is published before a relevant event, you can critique it because it is only partially relevant. For example, a journal article on the extension of parental rights was published in 2022. However, a major law was enacted in 2023; this new law was impactful and led to significant changes. In 2025, the article that was published in 2022 is only partially relevant because it did not account for the changes brought by the new legislation.
Examples:

- *Huda's analysis of reform of parental rights is limited because it was published before the Parental Rights Act 2023 was enacted.*
- *Abraham's study was lightly used because it was published before the recommendations of the Munro review were implemented.*
- *Despite its comprehensive analysis, this text failed to capture critical updates that emerged in the last decade.*
- *The theoretical framework used in Orlan's paper has been largely superseded by important updates and amendments.*

There are several events that can render texts partially irrelevant; new legislation, government reviews, post-Covid-19, new census, new statistics, change of government, financial crashes, tragedies, referendums, etc. If your text was published after such events, you can criticize the text for being limited. This demonstrates to the marker that you are aware of the context that surrounds the text. You are showing awareness of what was happening before and after the article was written. Journal articles are not written in a vacuum; they exist in particular contexts. Therefore, using this criticism indicates that you have not only read the article, but you have also read around the article.
Examples:

- *Johnson's article on working from home cultures was published a few months before the Covid-19 lockdowns, which significantly changed the landscape.*
- *The conclusions drawn in this article are based on the census datasets that were available at the time.*

There is another benefit of using this approach; you will provide your dissertation/research with a rationale. Your rationale is that your dissertation/research is a much-needed update. This gives your work much more significance.

Examples:

- *This study provides a much-needed updated from Lewis's study (2019), incorporating the latest data and research findings from the past three years.*
- *This study introduces recent insights and innovations that significantly advance the understanding established by Frank et al. (2020).*
- *Our work builds on Simpson's foundational research (2015) but provides a crucial update by incorporating the latest trends and emerging issues in the field.*

30 Critiquing academic texts using race, class or gender

If a text fails to sufficiently account for race, class, gender, neurodiversity, age, disability, etc., you can criticize it. For example, the text discusses human activity or matters that interact with human activity, but it does not sufficiently account for race, gender, class, neurodiversity, age, disability, etc. Instead, it presents a neutral or universal account. You can criticize the text on this basis because there are seldom human-related issues in which race, gender or class is not a significant factor. This line of argument challenges the notion of a universal student, a decontextualized organization or an abstract manager.

Examples:

- *Jones fails to acknowledge the significance of gender in this issue.*
- *The author overlooks the fact that race contributes to the highest rate of …*
- *Another weakness is that we are given no explanation of how social deprivation impacts.*
- *This research does not consider pre-existing tensions of gender and …*
- *By not addressing gender differences, Henry (2022) overlooks critical variations that could significantly influence his findings.*
- *By not incorporating neurodivergence as a critical factor, the study provides an incomplete and potentially misleading picture.*
- *The lack of consideration for religious affiliation weakens the study's applicability to diverse populations.*

It is important to expand this criticism by explaining why omitting race, gender, class, neurodiversity, age, disability, etc., is problematic; why does it negatively impact the text?

- You can argue that it was a missed opportunity to identify and highlight disparities and inequalities, which are essential for addressing and rectifying social injustices.
- You can argue that the author failed to provide a more holistic and nuanced understanding of the subject matter.
- You can argue that actionable recommendations or targeted interventions are difficult to achieve without a consideration of protected characteristics.
- You can argue that failing to consider race, gender and class can result in marginalization through adopting a one-size-fits-all approach.

Part 6

How to incorporate theories, models, concepts and frameworks into your assignment

31 Incorporating theories, concepts, frameworks and models into your writing

This section will show you how to incorporate models, theories, frameworks and concepts into your assignment. Their incorporation is crucial to provide a structured approach to analyse and interpret information. They offer an organized way to break down complex issues into manageable parts. Additionally, their use demonstrates scholarly engagement; you are not merely presenting opinions but are critically engaging with literature. This section will cover two areas:

- How to incorporate theories, concepts, frameworks and models into your assignments
- How to criticize theories, concepts, frameworks and models

By experimenting with approaches detailed in this section, you ensure that your work is well-founded, and of high academic quality. Additionally, when using these approaches, it is safer to confine yourself to theories, concepts, frameworks and models that were covered in your lectures or are mentioned in core reading lists.

What are theories, concepts, models and frameworks?

Theories are well-substantiated explanations of matters that occur in our everyday lives. We can define concepts as the softer form of theories because they have less of an evidence base; they are basic ideas or constructs that help us to understand the world. Models are simplified representations of reality that are used to explain, predict or manage complex phenomena. We can define frameworks as a structured way to understand and analyse complex issues. Both frameworks and models are usually illustrated.

Essentially, theories, concepts, frameworks and models offer us a simplification of the real world in order for us to understand what is happening in this real world. This is because the real world is chaotic, anarchic and constantly moving, all of which makes it difficult to study, so in response, we develop theories, concepts, frameworks and models to slow down the real world so that we can make sense of all its movements. To find definitions of models, frameworks, theories and concepts, please refer to page 16.

The diagram below illustrates our need for theories, concepts, frameworks and models.

| This realistic London Tube map is a metaphor of the real world. It is messy, complex and cluttered. It is difficult to grasp what is happening. | This stylized London Tube map is a metaphor of theories, concepts, frameworks and models. It is significantly more useful than the realistic map. |

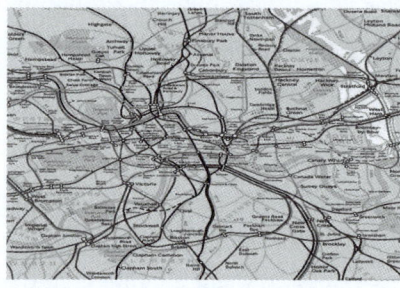
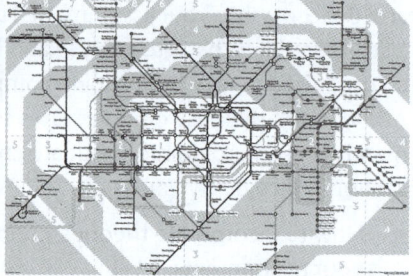

There are three approaches to incorporating models, frameworks, theories and concepts into your assignments:

Approach 1: Break it down

Approach 2: Broader significance

Approach 3: The ideal

Approach 1: Break it down

This approach requires you to structure your writing in accordance with the different aspects of a model, framework, theory or concept. Scholars have broken down their models, frameworks, theories and concepts into aspects, steps, stages, phases or tenets to make them easier to understand and apply. Therefore, we do not have to apply a model, framework, theory or concept in one go; we can apply it in a piecemeal way, one aspect, step, stage, phase or tenet at a time.

There are six simple steps of this approach:

1. **Intention:** State what you intend to do with the model, framework, theory or concept. For example, you state that you will use the model to chart the growth of Amazon, analyse the stages of the parliamentary law-making process, or investigate the manifestations of problematic behaviour, etc.

2. **Justification:** Provide a justification for using the model, framework, theory or concept. You could have chosen any model, framework,

theory or concept, but you chose a specific one – justify your choice. Your justification can be generic, for example:

- *This framework provides a structured approach to analyse and interpret information.*
- *This model breaks down complex issues into manageable parts.*
- *This concept provides a bridge from the assignment topic to established knowledge.*
- *This theoretical framework enables us to gain new insights.*
- *This model allows us to 'zoom out' to gain a comprehensive understanding of the topic.*

However, it is better to be more specific, your reason should draw from the specific characteristics of model, framework, theory or concept. For example:

- *Shelly's ladder of participation model was selected because it is centred on the redistribution of power.*

3. **Description:** Briefly describe the model, framework, theory or concept.
4. **Definition:** Then define the first step, stage, phase or tenet of the model, framework, theory or concept. For example:

    - *The first stage of Tuckman's framework is the forming stage of team development in which team members are usually excited to be part of the team and eager about the work ahead.*

5. **Connection:** Connect the first step, stage, phase or tenet to your assignment topic. For example:

    - *This stage of the Tuckman's model is similar to what was observed in the formation of tech startups.*
    - *This aspect of the framework is exemplified by …*
    - *This phase is evident in the case of …*
    - *This stage can be clearly seen in the case of …*

6. **Summary:** Summarize how the model, framework, theory or concept has contributed to understanding the topic or highlight any related implications or recommendations. For example:

    - *The use of this model revealed that participation in local government development projects was extremely limited and did little for the redistribution of power.*
    - *The model facilitated a clearer focus on the most crucial elements of occupational health and safety by simplifying the workplace environment.*

- *The interdisciplinary basis of this model enhanced our understanding of workplace stress through incorporating insights from public health and organizational psychology.*
- *The use of the concept helped delineate the boundaries of corporate manslaughter.*
- *Using the concept enabled us to focus on the key considerations of rehabilitating young offenders.*

Example: The break-it-down approach

This section will utilize Arnstein's ladder of citizen participation (2012) to assess the extent that local government housing developments engage with the public. This model was selected because it directs attention to genuine and meaningful participation, which is the foundation for the redistribution of power. Arnstein uses the metaphor of a ladder to describe graduations of citizen participation in urban programmes. The ladder has eight rungs, each corresponding to the extent of citizen power in determining the end product. The bottom rung of Arnstein's ladder is manipulation. Manipulation is at the bottom of the ladder where people have the impression that their views are taken on board, when in fact they are ignored. This rung resembles the predominant arrangements of local government housing developments (Simpson, 2023). While local government is outwardly involving citizens by holding public meetings, the participation appears to be superficial because there is minimal evidence of public contributions influencing the decision-making process (Simpson, 2023).

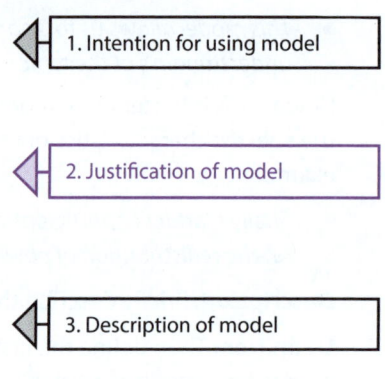

1. Intention for using model
2. Justification of model
3. Description of model
4. Definition of stage
5. Connection to your assignment topic

The next rung on the ladder is therapy. Arnstein (2012) explains that group therapy is masked as citizen participation. The real objective is not to enable participation but to enable powerholders to 'educate' or 'cure' the participants.

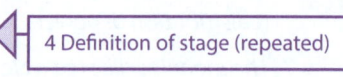

4 Definition of stage (repeated)

This rung is also found in local government projects in which citizens are invited to participate in committees, but the intent is to educate and engineer their support.

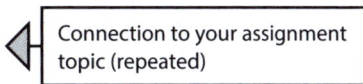

Utilizing Arnstein's ladder of participation revealed the lack of genuine participation in local government housing developments. It enabled this study to look past the superficial arrangements of local government to reveal the failure to engage with local communities and subject the citizens to clinical group therapy.

The next rung on the ladder is informing …

As the above example shows, you do not have to discuss every step, stage, phase or tenet of the model, framework, theory or concept. In the example, only two aspects of Arnstein's ladder of participation were discussed (manipulation and therapy). However, if you choose to only discuss two or three aspects, you should explicitly state that you are only discussing the aspects that are most relevant to your assignment.

Approach 2: Broader significance

This approach gives your writing broader significance by connecting it with models, frameworks, theories and concepts. Most of what we write in assignments are not isolated incidents, we can connect them to models, frameworks, theories and concepts. They are not just statistics; we can connect them to broader trends identified in models, frameworks, theories and concepts. They are not just random structures or behaviours; we can find them modelled in models, frameworks, theories and concepts. They are not new developments, we can find their patterns in models, frameworks, theories and concepts. This approach has a general appeal to whoever wants to enhance their academic writing.

This approach consists of two parts that form one paragraph:

1. **Assignment information:** This is information specific to your assignment; it could be your description of an occurrence, statistics, observation, etc.
2. **Connection to a relevant model, framework, theory or concept:** You establish a connection from the assignment information to a relevant model, framework, theory or concept. Alternatively, you can also

connect your assignment information to a scholarly comment, it does not necessarily have to be a model, framework, theory or concept.

Example connection sentences:

- *The rising trend of interactive whiteboards supports the theory of …*
- *The miscommunication between team members can be analysed using the model of …*
- *Remote work can be understood through the lens of …*
- *The fluctuation in commodity prices during this period reflects the principles of …*
- *The shift in voter behaviour reflects elements of …*

Example: The 'broader significance' approach

The lecture format gives very little room for dialogue. Lectures are usually delivered in a lecture theatre, which denote lecturer-centred didactic instruction in which students are passive learners in fixed rows of seating facing the instructor. This approach to teaching is what Turner (2017, p. 164) describes as a 'teacher-centred, transmission approach'. This approach depicts the role of the teacher as the transmitter of information to passive students. Turner's idea was developed from Freire's (1972, p. 32) earlier notion of the banking concept of education, which depicts the teacher as the knowledgeable narrator 'depositing' information into the 'empty' student.

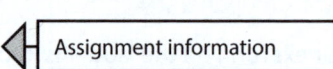
Assignment information

Connection to model, framework, theory or concept to show the broader significance of the above assignment information.

Approach 3: The ideal

This approach directs attention to a model, framework, theory or concept that represents the ideal situation. For example, you may have identified a problem or a situation that can be improved, so you will point to a model, framework, theory or concept as an example to be followed.

This approach consists of four parts that form one paragraph:

1. Indicate either a problem or situation that can be enhanced.
2. Direct the reader's attention to a model, framework, theory or concept.

Incorporating theories, concepts, frameworks and models into your writing

Example sentences that direct the reader's attention to a model, framework, theory or concept:

- *The issues with customer retention can be mitigated by adopting the model of …*
- *Implementing Kotter's 8-Step Change Model will provide a structured approach to managing …*
- *To address the declining employee engagement, we can apply the concept of …*
- *To improve outcomes, we can utilize the theory of …*

3. Justify why this model, framework, theory or concept is suitable to address the problem or enhance the scenario.
4. Describe the model, framework, theory or concept.

Example of the 'ideal'

Such organizations are likely to suffer from declining employee morale, low engagement levels and high turnover rates (Arthur, 2017). 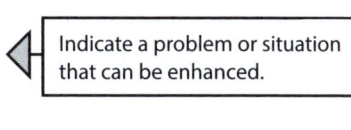 Indicate a problem or situation that can be enhanced.

This can be avoided by adopting Kotter's 8-Step Change Model. 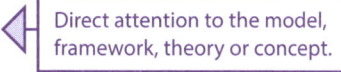 Direct attention to the model, framework, theory or concept.

Kotter's model was selected because it has attracted a body of supporting literature that focuses on instituting organizational change in a constantly shifting world. 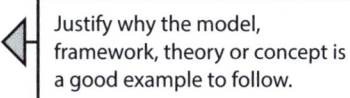 Justify why the model, framework, theory or concept is a good example to follow.

Building on Lewin's model, Kotter (1995; 1996) identified eight steps for managers to follow for successful organizational change. The first step for managers is …  Describe the model, framework, theory or concept.

32 Critiquing models, frameworks, theories and concepts

Whenever you engage with a model, framework, theory or concept, it is important to critique it. This is because models, frameworks, theories and concepts are a simplification of the real world, they are largely accurate, but they are *not* the real world. Therefore, there will be some degree of misalignment with the real world. Going back to the metaphor of the London Tube map, which is a stylized and simplified diagram. Stations may appear to be close together, but in reality, they are actually several miles apart. To find criticisms of models, frameworks, theories and concepts, refer to page 18.

There are three approaches to critiquing models, frameworks, theories and concepts. These approaches are akin to automobile services. We can either repair, enhance by using external parts, or completely scrap them.

Approach 1: Repair

We can make a slight repair or adjustment to models, frameworks, theories and concepts to ensure that they align with our current needs. This will be an update to make sure it is in line with current practice/research or an adjustment to suit a specific context. Essentially, you explicitly state that, as a whole, the model, framework, theory or concept is still useful, but there is a slight update, modification or adjustment that needs to be made to bring it line with a specific purpose. This may involve omitting or adding steps, stages, phases or tenets, adjusting the language or using a framework in a completely new context, which it was not initially designed for. Although there is a plethora of ways to repair models, frameworks, theories and concepts; you must explain two matters, in no particular order:

1. Explain what you have repaired (added, omitted, updated or modified).

2. Explain your reasoning for repairing the model, framework, theory or concept. The more substantial the repair, the more substantial the reasoning. If possible, cite a source of your reasoning.

Critiquing models, frameworks, theories and concepts

Example 1 of 'repair'

This study has utilized Bloom's taxonomy to categorize learning online. However, the first level of 'Remembering' has been replaced with 'Bookmarking/Favouriting'; this is where the students bookmark websites, resources and files for later use. This modification to Bloom's taxonomy was carried out because it better reflects the type of learning needed for the digital environment. The original and revised taxonomy was developed for traditional classroom practices, behaviours and actions, but does not account for the new behaviours, actions and learning opportunities emerging as technology advances and becomes more ubiquitous. Additionally, 'remembering' was too firmly placed in the cognitive domain, in contrary, 'bookmarking/favouriting' represents the delegation of our mental processes to digital devices (Church, 2019; Siemens and Downes, 2020).

> Explain what you have added, omitted, updated or modified.

> Explain your reasoning for repairing the model, framework, theory or concept.

Example 2 of 'repair'

Environment fit (EF) is a broad concept, incorporating both subjective and objective experiences, multiple levels of the environment, and a wide array of dimensions upon which comparisons are made (John, 2010). However, there is a minimal focus on time. Therefore, the impact of time has been enhanced in this assignment. As shown in Figure 32.1, time is seen through two lenses; clock time, defined as the linear and objective passage of time that can be measured, and psychological time representing a personal subjective view of time (Bluedorn and Denhardt, 1988; McGrath and Rotchford, 1983). This omission of time is curious given that time plays an important role in how PE is perceived and experienced. To this point, Murray (1938, p. 49) states, 'Man is not a

> Explain what you have added, omitted, updated or modified.

> Explain your reasoning for repairing the model, framework, theory or concept.

mere creature of the moment ... what he does is related not only to the settled past but also to shadowy preconceptions of what lies ahead.' When this time is ignored, we neglect the important role that context plays in defining experience (Kozlowski, 2009).

In relation to the above example, if possible, illustrate your repair of the model, framework, theory or concept. This will help with clarity and demonstrates your creativity. Label your illustration and dedicate a section to describing it in detail.

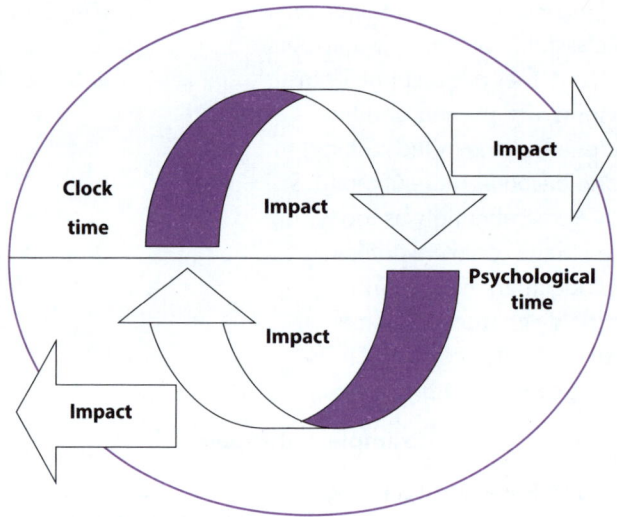

Figure 6.1 A revised EF construct with a focus on how time impacts context and process

Approach 2: Enhance with foreign parts

In this approach, you have found a model, framework, theory or concept to use in your assignment. However, you realize that there is a limitation with your chosen model, framework, theory or concept, therefore, you look elsewhere for a suitable part from another model, framework, theory or concept. It is essentially a merger between two models, frameworks, theories or concepts.

The motivation to search elsewhere stems from your opinion that your chosen model, framework, theory or concept is salvageable; even though it lacks something, it can still be useful. Therefore, rather than scrap it, you seek out complementary models, frameworks, theories and concepts to strengthen it or make it more relevant to your assignment question. Using this approach, you must explain five matters, in no particular order:

1. Explain which two models, frameworks, theories or concepts you merged together.
2. Explain your reasoning for merging the two models, frameworks, theories or concepts. Although not necessary, your reasoning will be strengthened if you cite a source.
3. (Optional) Explain a limitation of merging two models, frameworks, theories or concepts.
4. (Optional) Explain how the limitation was overcome or mitigated. Fundamentally, you want to argue that the limitation that you identified does not detract from the benefits of merging the two models, frameworks, theories or concepts.
5. If possible, illustrate your merged models, frameworks, theories or concepts.

Example of 'enhance with foreign parts'

This study will develop a framework derived from the person–environment (PE) and self-regulation literature to better understand how employees fit within their work environment. It is puzzling why there has not been an attempt to fully merge PE literature and theories of self-regulation. The PE literature has much to benefit from self-regulation theories because the latter is the leading paradigm for understanding employee behaviour (Johnson, 2008; Smith, 2013). Moreover, there are many parallels between them. The most significant parallel is that they are both inexorably intertwined because ideal–experienced discrepancies are at the heart of both self-regulation theories and PE theories. Explain which two models, frameworks, theories or concepts you merged together. Note: Sometimes, models, concepts, theories and frameworks are referred to as 'literature'. For example, 'PE theories' will also be called 'PE literature'.

 Explain your reasoning for merging the two models, frameworks, theories or concepts.

However, this merger has a limitation; the framework only captures self-regulatory processes in the work environment of individuals, it is less informative for understanding how it relates to social collectives like work teams and organizations. Given that the Explain a limitation of merging two models, frameworks, theories or concepts.

 Explain how the limitation was overcome or mitigated.

assignment question does not cover this aspect, the approach is still valid. Moreover, the merger has helped identify promising directions for future research.

Approach 3: 'Write-off'

This approach criticizes the model, framework, theory or concept to the extent that it cannot be salvaged. It is beyond repair; it cannot be enhanced with foreign parts, it is to be left alone because it is inaccurate, outdated, problematic, overly complex, overly simple, etc. This approach is more effective when the criticism is based on scholarly sources. If you need help finding scholarly sources to criticize models, frameworks, theories and concepts, refer to page 18.

Using this approach, you must include three matters:

1. Outline the benefits of the model, framework, theory or concept.
2. Outline the limitations of the model, framework, theory or concept.
3. State your verdict on the model, framework, theory or concept. You conclude that the cons outweigh the pros; although the model, framework, theory or concept may have some useful aspects, its problems outweigh its benefits.

Example of 'write-off'

In its simplest form, it is understandable why Lewin's model attracted so much attention. It helps teams identify the problem, have everyone appreciate the problem, identify a new paradigm to replace the old problem and solidify that into place. If practice follows theory, Lewin's model is one of the most effective organizational change models available and one of the easiest to implement. Outline the benefits of the model, framework, theory or concept.

However, actual life is not entirely logical. Humphries (2015) argues that the complexities of organizational life create several problems for Lewin's model. If, for example, change is required not because of an existing problem but because changes in technology require a completely new process, Outline the limitations of the model, framework, theory or concept.

Lewin's 'unfreezing' stage may be compromised. It is after all difficult to 'unfreeze' something that did not previously exist. A final common criticism of Lewin's model is that his model fails to understand that most organizations need to change constantly, which means refreezing will inevitably become the beginning of the next cycle seeking to 'unfreeze' again (Jones, 2013; Williams, 2008).

If the criticism was directed at just one aspect of Lewin's model, it may have been possible to 'repair' it or at least salvage it through conjoining it to other change models. However, problems exist throughout all stages of Lewin's model.

State your verdict on the model, framework, theory or concept.

Part 7

How to reflect critically

Critical reflection

A reflective assignment is where students are assessed on their ability to write about their experiences, considering what they have learned, how they have changed, and how these experiences might influence their future actions. Reflections may be in an essay format, oral presentation or a journal entry. You are encouraged to present reflective accounts subjectively. You are not an impartial observer; you are an active participant.

Critical reflection goes one step beyond the normal reflection; it is the process of analysing, questioning and evaluating your own thoughts, actions, experiences and beliefs, with the aim of gaining deeper understanding, improving future practices and fostering personal and professional growth. It involves going beyond surface-level thinking to examine the underlying assumptions, values and biases that influence one's behaviour and decisions. If you are able to demonstrate critical reflection, your grades will significantly increase.

This 'critical' aspect of reflection is the most difficult aspect of reflective writing. Therefore, this section will provide you with various approaches to make your reflections more critical.

33. Using reflective models to structure your writing

34. Zooming out to the wider literature

35. Choosing between two paths

36. Articulating doubt

37. Creating themes from your reflection

38. Bad practice vs best practice

39. Incorporating statements into your reflection

40. Incorporating different perspectives into your reflection

41. Uncovering power in your reflection

As with all hacks or approaches in this book, you can tweak them to suit your circumstances, or you can merge approaches together.

33 Using reflective models to structure your writing

If you are asked to reflect on your experiences, you should consider using a reflective model. This will enhance the criticality of your writing because it connects your reflective writing with the literature and provides you with a structure to organize your thoughts and feelings in a coherent and critical way.

Scholars have designed reflective models as a series of steps or stages. Their models contain 'empty' categories that require you to 'fill' them with your thoughts, actions, experiences and beliefs. These models will help you view a specific situation from multiple angles. For example, Driscoll's 'What' model requires you to reflect on a specific situation from three angles. The first angle is 'What happened?'; this is where you describe a specific situation and its context. The second angle is 'So what?'; this is where you discuss the significance of the situation; what did you learn as a result of the situation? The third angle is 'Now what?'; this is where you think about the future action that you will take to remedy such situations.[1]

There is a plethora of reflective models to choose from; to find an overview of models developed by scholars, simply type 'reflective models' into the Google search engine.

Only visit the search results from universities. Several universities have produced overviews of reflective models. Browse through the models to see which is best for your needs.

There are six simple steps of using a reflective model in your assignment

1. **Intention:** State what you intend to do with the reflective model. For example:

   This assignment will utilize Kolb's Experiential Learning Cycle to reflect on a disciplinary meeting at my workplace.

---

[1] Driscoll, J. (ed.) (2007), *Practicing Clinical Supervision: A Reflective Approach for Healthcare Professionals*, Edinburgh: Elsevier.

2. **Justification:** Provide a justification for using the reflective model. You could have chosen any reflective model, but you chose a specific reflective model – justify your choice. For example:
   - *I opted for Gibbs's Reflective Cycle because it provides a structured approach to reflection, allowing me to analyse each stage of my experience, from description to action planning.*
   - *I chose Kolb's Experiential Learning Cycle because it emphasizes the iterative process of learning through one's experience, making it ideal for understanding how I can apply what I've learned in future situations.*
   - *Schon's Reflective Practice was selected because it focuses on reflection-in-action and reflection-on-action, which are crucial for real-time problem-solving and retrospective learning in my current role.*
   - *I chose Johns' Model of Structured Reflection because it encourages deep, structured analysis of the situation, integrating both personal and professional insights into my reflective process.*
   - *I applied Borton's Developmental Framework as it provides a straightforward yet comprehensive method of reflection, which aligns well with my need to systematically evaluate my actions and their outcomes.*

3. **Description:** Provide an overview of the reflective model. Refer to page 16 to find definitions/overviews of reflective models.

4. **Critique:** Critique the reflective model. This should not be a total or devasting criticism of the model because if the criticism is too heavy, the marker will question why you selected the model. All that is needed is a minor criticism to demonstrate critical analysis and your acknowledgement that no reflective model is perfect. As discussed, all models are simplifications of the real world; although they resemble real-world processes, they can never capture the complexities and messiness of the real world. Although not completely necessary, try to find criticisms of reflective model from academic sources. To find such criticisms, refer to page 18. Alternatively, type 'criticism' and the name of the reflective model into the Google search engine to find journal articles and webpages from universities and reputable organizations. If you are unable to find criticisms, here are some examples:
   - *Johns' model of structured reflection has been regarded as overly detailed to the extent that it imposes a framework that is external to the practitioner, leaving little scope for inclusion of his/her own approach.*[2]

---

[2] Davies, C., Finlay, L. and Bullman, A. (eds) (2005), *Changing Practice in Health and Social Care*, London: Sage.

- *There is very little in Gibbs's Reflective Cycle to encourage the reflector to challenge values or assumptions associated with any of their actions in the experience.*
- *Kolb's model is too individualistic; it is based on the notion of experience as a phenomenon of the individual, rather than connected to the experiences of others.*[3]

5. **Overcoming criticism:** Explain how you overcame the above criticism; how did you mitigate the above criticism to ensure that the reflective model was still useful? For example, a criticism of Johns's Model is that it is overly complex, thus, a response to this criticism is to explain that you spent more time contextualizing and reinterpreting the stages in order to internalize the framework and make it more relevant to your professional practice. A criticism of Gibbs's Model is the lack of scope to challenge values or assumptions, thus, a response to this criticism is to explain that you used the 'analysis' stage of Gibbs's Cycle to challenge your values and assumptions. Also, you can explain that you incorporated this textbook's approach to critical reflection to enhance this section. A criticism of Kolb's model is that it is too individualistic; thus, a response to this criticism is to explain that you used this textbook's heteroglossia approach to bring in different voices.

6. **Stage-by-stage:** Define the first stage of the reflective model, then 'fill' the stage with your reflections. Define the second stage of the reflective model, then 'fill' the stage with your reflections. Carry on this process for every stage of the reflective model. This stage-by-stage section of your reflection is the most important.

Example of a using a reflective model

This assignment will utilize Gibbs's Reflective Cycle to reflect on a disciplinary meeting at my workplace. I opted for Gibbs' Reflective Cycle because it provides a structured approach to reflection, allowing me to analyse each stage of my experience, from description to action planning. Gibbs's Reflective Cycle was developed by Graham Gibbs to give structure to learning from experiences over a course of six stages. It must be noted that he received some criticism; Arthur (2025) observed that the cycle does not provide a space for the reflector to challenge

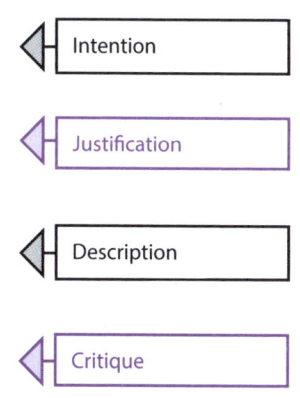

Intention

Justification

Description

Critique

---

[3]Moon, J. (2005), *Handbook of Reflective and Experiential Learning*, Abingdon: RoutledgeFalmer.

their values or assumptions. This limitation is addressed through using the 'analysis' stage to challenge my values and assumptions. Also, I have incorporated Arthur's approaches to critical reflection to enhance the articulation of my challenges.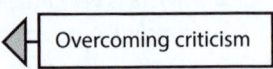
The first stage of Gibbs's Cycle is description. In this section, we are prompted to describe a critical incident in detail. My critical incident was my summoning to a disciplinary meeting at my workplace where I was …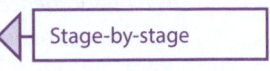

34 Zooming out to the wider literature

Critical reflection requires you to *zoom in* to a specific situation that is personal to you, then to *zoom out* of that situation to get a broader understanding of what is happening on a larger scale. By zooming out, you will be able to see the bigger picture. For example, when you zoom out of an incident that impacted you at work, you realize that it was not an isolated incident, many others have been impacted by similar incidents. What you experienced is part of a broader trend that has impacted others, the details may vary, but there are striking similarities. Most of what you experience in your personal life has been the subject of study, research and policy from scholars, governments and non-governmental organizations. Thus, zooming out is drawing from this body of literature to generalize your personal experiences.

In your reflective writing, there are five circumstances to zoom out to see the bigger picture

1. **Problem or issue:** If you express in your reflection that you encountered a problem or an ongoing issue, you can zoom out to explain how prevalent the problem or issue is in the wider world. These problems or issues are largely outside your control; they can be organizational, operational or environmental.

Example of problem or issue

For past few years, my workload at the care home has increased. I am having to do additional work due to significant staff shortages. Unfortunately, this is not an isolated incident. In England, the vacancy rate in the adult social care workforce for 2022–23 was 9.9 per cent. There were staffing problems in the UK care sector well before Covid. However, the pandemic exacerbated the crisis (Orlando, 2024).

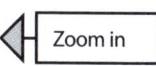

2. **Intense feelings:** If you express in your reflection that you felt intense feelings/emotions or some form of internal wrangling because of a situation, you can zoom out to connect your personal situation to the academic literature. Much of what we think, and feel has been an object of study and concern. From feelings of discrimination to emotions felt from workplace bullying, there is a body of literature that speaks to our personal experiences.

Example of intense feelings

When I looked around at the members of the board, I didn't see anyone that looked like me. Even though I had the qualifications and experience to match most of the executive team, I have always felt inadequate. My feelings of inadequacy bear a resemblance to what Frimpong (2015) describes as 'imposter syndrome', which is a feeling that one isn't good enough and doesn't belong despite evidence to the contrary. Imposter syndrome is often defined as a 'failure of rationality' and as an 'illusion of personal incompetence' (Smith, 2010, p. 45).

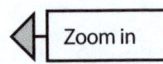

3. **Change of procedure:** If you express in your reflection that you had underwent a change of procedure at your workplace or received training to accommodate a change, you can zoom out to broader market conditions, national controversies, protest movements, legal or regulatory directives that prompted your organization to change.

Example of change of procedure

On that day, I had to undergo cybersecurity training to increase my awareness of phishing scams and the importance of strong passwords and multi-factor authentication (MFA). It appears that this is part of a wider response to the increasing frequency and sophistication of cyber-attacks that have driven organizations to invest more in cybersecurity training for their staff (Jones, 2025).

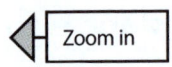
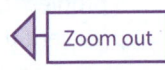

4. **Organizational structure:** If you describe the organizational structure in which you work, study or volunteer, you can zoom out to relate it broader patterns of organization.

Example of organizational structure

I felt that there was minimal freedom given to me. Even though I had the experience, and I was mostly 'on the ground', everything had to go through central management. This is similar to what Mason (2002) referred to as 'centralisation of decision-making', which is a hierarchical organizational structure whereby ultimate power and decision-making is concentrated at the top rather than shared with lower levels of the organization.

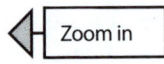
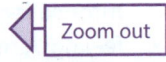

5. **Behaviour:** If you describe a particular behaviour from an individual or a group, you can zoom out to relate it the academic literature.

Example of behaviour

She implemented the strategy even though she was adamant that it wouldn't work. This was curious to me; however, it appears that the environment that we inhabit influences such behaviours, there is a body of literature on 'situationism' which proposes that strong situations exert pressure on individuals to behave in a certain way. Our individual patterns of thoughts, feelings and behaviours are suppressed to the extent that 'a health care practitioner will use an evidence-based intervention, programme or service despite being sceptical of its merits' (Johnson, 2017, p. 36).

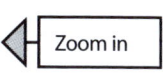

35 Choosing between two paths

Rather than presenting a smooth and unblemished reflection, it is important to show some degree of tension or conflict. The Two Path approach requires you reflect on a significant moment in your life where you faced two distinct paths and had to choose one. This reflection should explore the reasoning behind your decision. This is a critical activity that sheds light on your decision-making process. These two distinct paths could be deciding whether to tell your manager what you actually think or tell your manager want she wants to hear; taking the advice of an expert in the field or following your heart; responding to an offensive statement in the moment or responding at a later time, etc. All these choices come with ramifications, which will impact our future selves. Moreover, choosing one of the two paths in front of us is not a simple choice between good or bad; it often comes down to choosing the lesser evil or the greater good.

The approach consists of four simple steps

1. **Introduction:** State that you had to make a choice between two matters.

    Example sentences:

    I found myself at a crossroads, where I had to make a choice between …

    I reached a point where I had to choose between … each with its own set of challenges and opportunities.

2. **Path 1:** Fully describe the first path and explain why it is appealing and unappealing.
3. **Path 2:** Fully describe the second path and explain why it is appealing and unappealing.
4. **Justify a path:** Select one of the paths, justify why you opted for a particular path. If possible, substantiate your justification with relevant literature.

Example of 'two paths'

Last year, I found myself standing at the crossroads where two paths became clear to me. I had to choose one; the decision weighed heavily on me. The first path was to accept the offer of promotion at my current workplace, which is growing a mid-sized tech company. This was an opportunity to gain additional responsibilities and enjoy a substantial salary increase. However, the problem with this path is that I am no longer passionate about this sector; the day-to-day realities of the job have eroded most of the mystique. In fact, a promotion would constrain doing the things I actually enjoy and increase tasks that are incredibly dull and repetitive. The second path was to accept an offer of an MSc in Organization Psychology. It is something that I am immensely interested in, and I can foresee a promising career in this area. However, this would mean turning down the promotion and reducing my working hours to pursue the MSc, this would mean that I am forsaking a stable career to venture into the unknown.

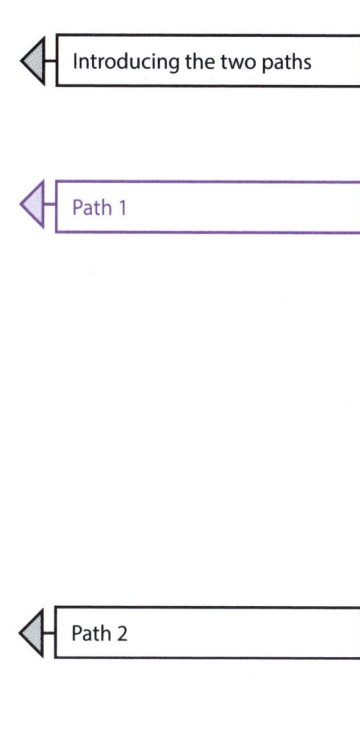

I opted for the MSc, it was a difficult choice, but I could not carry on feeling unfulfilled. I embraced the 'passion principle', which is the prioritization of personally fulfilling work even at the expense of job security or a decent salary (Mills, 2010). Also, this decision gave me the confidence to 'shrink the footprint', which means shrinking the space that full-time work takes up to open more time and energy to do things that we enjoy; switching part-time hours made my job role bearable (Schneider, 2017).

36 Articulating doubt

When you articulate doubt or uncertainty about a specific situation, you demonstrate self-awareness and critical thinking. It shows that you are in a state of questioning and reflecting on different perspectives, which is key to producing a highly graded reflective assignment. Articulating doubt also distinguishes your assignment from others because it showcases your authenticity and honesty; we all experience doubt even in concrete matters. Such displays make your reflection more meaningful and credible, as they reflect the genuine challenges and thought processes that we all experience.

An Illustration of our back-and-forth processing

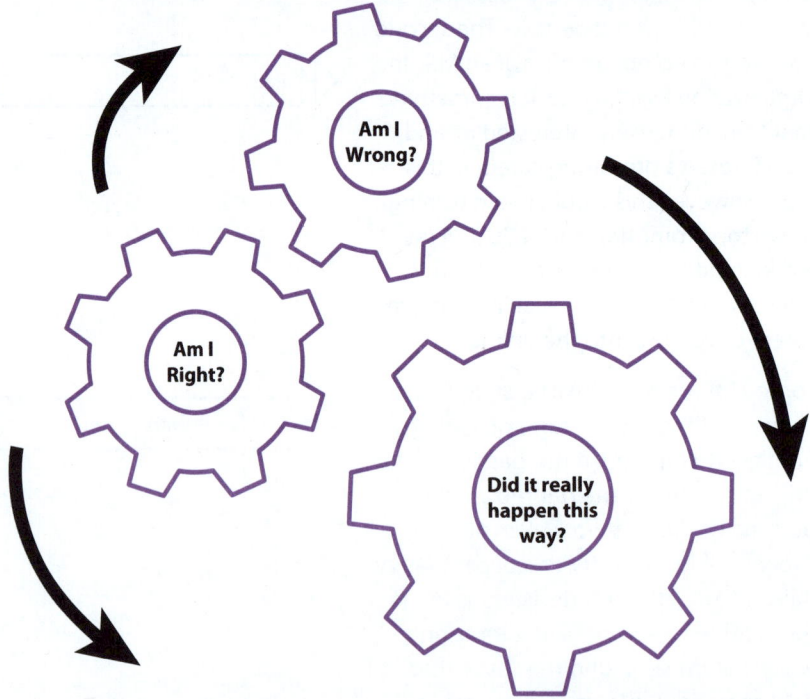

In order to articulate doubt in writing, we must simulate the back-and-forth processing of information. A metaphor for this is that a raw product enters the assembly line, then the wheels of doubt and counterargument start to turn to process this product until we get an ultra-processed product at the end. Likewise, the initial thought enters our heads, then we process this thought, it changes shape and form because of our questioning and doubting until we get a final thought, which we settle on. This is the spirit of how we write about our wrestling with doubt.

You can use this approach to discuss numerous situations; you may have had initial thoughts about your manager, then reflecting on your exchanges with your manager, you gradually start to doubt your initial thoughts and develop a more refined conception of her. Another example is how you feel about your managerial capabilities; you were initially very pleased with them but reflecting on a series of past events and anxious about future events, you conclude that you are a good manager only in certain contexts.

The approach consists of four simple steps

1. **State the initial thought:** Fully describe your initial thought. This description must be expressed with absolute clarity. It is important that it is a single thought about a specific situation.

2. **Doubt creeps in:** Your initial thought is confronted with doubts. The doubts are the reasons that erode the certainty of your initial thought.

    Example sentences:

    - *As I began to question certain assumptions, my doubts began to reshape my initial thoughts on …*
    - *I encountered doubts that led me to reconsider …*
    - *My growing doubts began to challenge my initial thoughts, prompting me to think more critically about the issue …*
    - *My initial thoughts have evolved due to the doubts.*
    - *Doubts played a crucial role in altering my initial thoughts on …*
    - *These uncertainties have forced me to re-evaluate my initial thoughts.*

3. **Pushback:** You hold firm to the initial thought and challenge the doubt by providing justification for your initial thought.

4. **Resolution:** Settle on a resolution that has been impacted by the back and forth; perhaps you compromise between the doubt and your initial thought, or you hang on to your initial thought in a moderated form, or you completely give in to the doubts.

Example of doubt

I attended an induction event for a new cohort of students, and the head of the department introduced me to the students as the new 'cool' teacher. This title of 'cool' was problematic to me; being 'cool' is on the long list of stereotypes attributed to black males (Henry, 2009). Conversely, what was wrong with being 'cool'? To be cool is a compliment. I started to suspect that I was overthinking the situation. Though stereotypical, being labelled 'cool' is not a negative stereotype. Moreover, I like the Head of the Department, we have always had a good rapport. I know what she said was meant to be a compliment; I don't believe it came from a bad place. Nonetheless, how do I know what she truly meant? I know what being 'cool' means in my specific cultural context, but what did that mean to her? Maybe she defines it as disinterested, nonchalant or unconcerned. I don't think I'm any of those things. Moreover, I am the only one who is being referred to as cool; everybody else was just referred to by their title. Then again, nobody looks like me in this department. I just want to be perceived as a normal lecturer, but it appears there is an 'asterisk next to the title of lecturer' (Webb et al., 2023, p. 23). I decided to keep it to myself, because I may be wrong and do not want to be perceived as the 'race' guy. Such matters are a 'distraction' that keep me from pursuing my goals (Morrison, 1993).

Annotations:
- **State the initial thought**
- **Doubt creeps in.** Words like 'conversely', 'however', 'nonetheless' signal a transition from one point of view to another.
- **Pushback**
- **Resolution**

As the example demonstrates, expressing doubt in your reflection is pitting two contrasting voices against each other.

37 Creating themes from your reflection

Creating themes from your reflections involves reflecting on a specific situation, then extracting key themes from that situation. For example, if you reflect on a Microsoft Teams meeting that you attended, you can extract key themes of 'remote work', 'online etiquette' and 'in-person communication vs online communication'. These three themes are three ways of looking at the Teams meeting. Instead of reflecting on the Teams meeting as a whole, it has been dissected into three neat portions, see Figure 7.1. This demonstrates your ability to organize and structure your reflections. It is also a critical activity; it goes back to the original usage of being critical, which meant 'to separate, to decide, to sieve.'

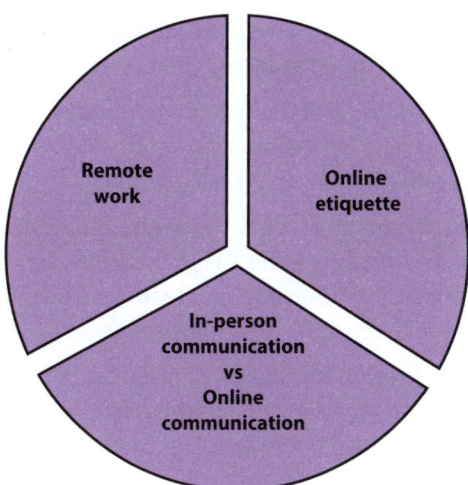

Figure 7.1 An Illustration of dissecting an experience into themes

To create themes, you should reflect on an experience, then consider keywords that best describes the experience; what are the headlines? What stuck out to you? These will be your themes. Once you have settled on your themes, you can connect these themes to the academic literature. For example, reflecting on a job interview experience, you extracted two themes: body language and preparedness. These two themes have much written about them; you can now connect your personal experiences of body language and preparedness to the wider academic literature.

The approach consists of five simple steps

1. **Introduction:** Inform the reader that you separated your reflection into themes. For example:
   - *I will explore my reflections by organizing them into several key themes.*
   - *My reflections will be discussed under several themes to provide a structured analysis of my first day at work.*
   - *To better articulate my thoughts, I will divide my reflections into five themes.*
   - *I will present my reflections through an exploration of several interconnected themes.*
   - *I will categorize my reflections into a series of thematic discussions.*
   - *For the sake of clarity, my reflections will be organized into several thematic areas.*

2. **Theme 1:** State the name of the first theme, describe the specific situation that inspired the theme, then, if possible, zoom out to connect the specific situation to the academic literature.

3. **Theme 2:** State the name of the second theme, describe the specific situation that inspired the theme, then, if possible, zoom out to connect the specific situation to the academic literature.

4. **Theme 3:** State the name of the third theme, describe the specific situation that inspired the theme, then, if possible, zoom out to connect the specific situation to the academic literature. (Note: If you have more than three themes, carry on with this format.)

5. **Closing unifying comment:** Write a concluding critical reflection to bring together all the themes. What is the relationship between the themes? What do the themes reveal? For example:
   - *When considered collectively, these themes reveal a deeper understanding of…*
   - *By bringing these themes together, we can see how they contribute to a more comprehensive view of…*
   - *The convergence of these themes points to the broader impact of…*
   - *Taken as a whole, these themes illustrate the multifaceted nature of…*
   - *In summary, these interconnected themes reveal the underlying reason of…*

Example of creating themes

I will present my reflections on my first year of university through an exploration of two interconnected themes. **Introduction**

The most prominent theme that comes out of my experience is anxiety. I felt considerable anxiety in my first year of study. I frequently doubted my abilities, fearing that I wasn't academically capable or socially adept enough to fit in. This anxiety manifested in various ways, from sleepless nights worrying about assignments to feeling isolated in social situations. It would appear that such feelings of anxiety are commonplace for first-year students; Martinez (2023) observed that first-year students are particularly prone to pressures to excel academically, make new friends, and establish a sense of identity, which can contribute to university students' anxiety.

First theme: In this section, name the theme, describe the personal experience that inspired the theme and connect it to the academic literature.

Additionally, the theme of belonging is something that shaped my initial experiences, I found myself questioning whether I truly belonged at university. Moving away from home and entering an entirely new environment, I was overwhelmed by the size of the university, and the pressure to establish new social connections. My difficulties with belonging prompted me to reflect on its importance. Pedler (2025) states that a sense of belonging is important as it incorporates feelings of being valued, included and accepted at university.

Second theme: In this section, name the theme, describe the personal experience that inspired the theme and connect it to the academic literature.

In summary, these interconnected themes reveal the importance of attending to specific needs of students very early in their journey.

Closing unifying comment

38 Bad practice vs best practice

This approach involves identifying bad practice or practice that can be enhanced and then recommending a better way. For example, your reflection identifies an organizational structure that inhibits innovation, so you recommend a better way of organizing that encourages innovation and growth. This better way that you recommend should be documented in the academic literature, organizational/governmental reports, or professional frameworks/charters. Essentially, you should juxtapose bad practice with best practice, see below:

Bad practice		Best practice
Lindon (2022) states that it is vital to place books throughout the setting in order to normalize reading.	vs	When I looked around the setting, I realized that the books were placed and used in one area of the setting.

Bad practice		Best practice
At the institute, there was no training provision that focused on interacting appropriately with neurodivergent service users.	vs	Recent guidance from the Care Quality Commission (CQC) (2025) requires Providers to ensure that all staff receive training in how to interact appropriately with people with a learning disability and autistic people, at a level appropriate to their role.

The approach consists of four simple steps

1. **Introduction:** Describe the bad practice or practice that can be enhanced. Examples of bad practice are micromanagement, lack of equity, diversity and inclusion, unclear communication, failure to get consent, neglecting safety protocols, ignoring customer feedback, lack of professional development, poor work-life balance, understaffing, lack of transparency, unethical practices, etc.

2. **Detriments of bad practice:** State the detriment(s) or potential detriment(s) of the bad practice that you observed. Examples of detriments are increased errors, low morale, fines and penalties, lawsuits, burnout, high staff turnover, reputational damage, negative reviews, loss of customers, supply chain issues, toxic work environment, missed opportunities, etc.

3. **Best practice:** Direct the reader's attention to a better way. Examples of best practice are patient-centred care, student-centred learning, user-centred design, diversity and inclusion initiatives, professional development programmes, effective and transparent communication, ethical sourcing, agile methodology, sustainable practices, ethical investment practices, etc.
4. **Benefits of best practice:** State the benefits of best practice.

Example of best practice vs bad practice

Throughout the week, I was shocked by the way the healthcare assistants conversed with the patients. It appeared that the patients' informational and emotional needs were unmet. This was problematic for several reasons. First, the communication issues created unnecessary stress and confusion for the patients. Second, it often led to distressed families of the patients contacting the care home. A way to remedy the flawed and problematic communication issues is by adopting Reese's (2009) patient-centred communication model, which rests on three principles; (1) eliciting and understanding patient perspectives (concerns, ideas, expectations, needs, feelings and functioning), (2) understanding the patient within his or her unique psychosocial and cultural contexts and (3) reaching a shared understanding of patient problems and the treatments that are concordant with patient values. There are several benefits of this model of communication. Reese (2009) observed a marked improvement in patient satisfaction, adherence to advice and health outcomes.

39 Incorporating statements into your reflection

This approach involves using statements from people or organizations. Incorporating statements into your reflection will enhance your reflection in several ways:

- It enhances authenticity and personalization by allowing you to express your thoughts, feelings and experiences in a way that feels natural. It can make the narrative more engaging and easier to follow.
- It can provide context for your reflections, making it clearer why certain events were significant to you.
- Many reflective models encourage you to reflect on interactions; we are not solitary creatures, we exist in social worlds.
- The last and most profound reason is that you can demonstrate critical analysis by analysing the words that were said to you. Words are rarely neutral, we can interpret them to reveal bias, context and deeper meaning. We can write many paragraphs explaining the meaning of just a few words. For example, in a reflection, a parent mentioned,

> 'There are only two universities in England.'

We can expand this statement by interpreting what the parent meant; it would seem that the two universities that they were referring to were Oxford and Cambridge. For centuries, England's two oldest institutions enjoyed a strict duopoly on higher learning, enforced by law. Therefore, according to the parent, universities which were established after these two are not legitimate universities or they are universities that should not be sought after. We can expand this statement further by highlighting such antiquated and elitist attitudes towards higher education. Additionally, we can expand the statement even further by looking at what constitutes a university. Thus, just from five words, we were able to provide extensive critical commentary.

It is important to note that the statement that you critically reflect on should be brief and relevant. Extensive statements will cause confusion and dilute the points you are trying to make. A statement should be no longer than a sentence; one to three statements in a typical reflective assignment is sufficient.

Additionally, when you interpret the words of others, you should use cautious words because you may be right or wrong.

For example, instead of writing,

What she meant was that he was too senior to help me move the furniture.

you could write instead,

What she possibly meant was that he was too senior to help me move the furniture.

Other cautious words are may; might; could; perhaps; probably; conceivably; feasibly; arguably; seems to; tends to; looks like; appears to show; indicates; signals; could be seen as.

Example of 'incorporating statements'

She turned to her assistant and yelled, 'I don't pay you to answer back to me.' This is one of many outbursts that I observed in the setting. Her interaction with her staff indicated three matters. The first of which was what Pizzolitto (2026) referred to as an 'authoritarian management style', which involves high levels of control over subordinates. Ensured by organizational hierarchies, authoritarian leaders tend to use their authority to demand absolute obedience of their followers (de Hoogh et al., 2023). Superiors adopting these leadership styles tend to centralize their power and accentuate the power distance between them and their subordinates (Schaubroeck et al., 2024). The second matter was that her outburst was an example of the prevalence of 'hierarchical communication' in the sector. Hierarchical communication reflects the hierarchal structure of command and control (Raith, 2022). Lastly, it would be unjust to depict the manager in such a bad light without talking about the context that prompted her behaviour. It has been well known for many years that stress can impact one's behaviour at work; unmanageable heavy workloads, higher job expectations, job insecurity can lead to significant stress, which results in the type of behaviour that I observed.

Statement

Analysis of statement
Rather than analyse the statement all at once, this example has focused on three aspects of the statement and discussed them one at a time. Also, the example showed two sides of the manager, it pointed to her problematic leadership style, but it also argued that she was a product of her environment.

40 Incorporating different perspectives into your reflection

This approach involves incorporating differing perspectives into your reflection by providing different points of view from people and/or organizations on a specific matter. You step into the shoes of others and speculate how they may view a specific matter.

An illustration of two perspectives looking at the same issue

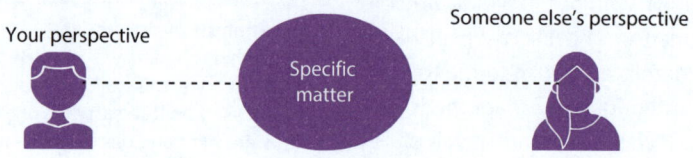

As the above illustration demonstrates, they are both looking at the same issue from different perspectives; the organization will view it in a particular way, and another person may have a differing perspective.

Since this approach involves speculation of perspectives other than your own, you should use cautious words (may; might; could; perhaps; probably; conceivably; feasibly; arguably; seems to; tends to; looks like; appears to show; indicates; signals; could be seen as). Another important point is that although you are discussing the perspectives of others, their perspectives should be matters relating to you. For example, their perspectives should relate to something you did, something you did not do, something that happened to you or your conduct. It is very easy to drift off and talk about other people, so remember that this is your reflection, so make sure that their perspectives are related to you or your actions.

There are two ways to incorporate differing perspectives into your reflection:

1. **Narrator view:** As the narrator, you have a bird's-eye view observing multiple perspectives on a specific matter. From party to party, you speculate what their perspectives could be. These perspectives could be drawn from a person, organization, department or collective, etc. You should try to limit the perspectives to two or three parties; if you describe too many perspectives, there is a chance that your assignment will become too convoluted.

2. **Back and forth:** You describe your perspective on a specific matter and juxtapose it with a differing perspective from another person, organization, a department or collective, etc. This is a back-and-forth exchange between your perspective and a counter perspective.

The 'narrator view' consists of four simple steps

1. **Overview of issue:** Introduce the issue and indicate that the issue is not seen in the same way by all parties.

    Example sentences:

    - *The proposed expansion of my company caused significant debate in the office.*
    - *The shopfloor staff were hopeful that it would lead to further opportunities, while their supervisors were deeply concerned about the impact on middle management.*
    - *My promotion prompted mixed reactions from the senior leadership team and my department.*
    - *My announcement of the revised remote work policies divided the company, with some employees overjoyed with the flexibility and work-life balance, while others felt that team were becoming distant from each other.*

2. **Perspective 1:** Introduce the first party, describe their unique viewpoint and speculate why they held that viewpoint.

3. **Perspective 2:** Introduce the second party, describe their unique viewpoint and speculate why they held that viewpoint.

4. **Narrator voice:** As the narrator with a bird's-eye view of the different perspectives, you have the final word. This can involve weighing up the perspectives to identify the most valid perspective and justifying how you reached this conclusion. Alternatively, you can explain what could have been done to rectify their misinterpretations of the matter.

Example of 'narrator view'

I was promoted to a senior role in a few months of my arrival to the company. This prompted mixed reactions from my colleagues. **Overview of issue:** Introduce the issue and indicate that the issue is not seen in the same way by all parties.

Some of my colleagues in the finance department seemed upset by the decision. I assume that their reaction was due to my short **Perspective 1:** Introduce the first party, describe their unique viewpoint and speculate why they held that viewpoint.

time at the company; many of them had been here for a longer time period and had not received such commendation. But I suspect most of the ire came from the belief that I was a 'diversity hire'. Regarding the senior leadership team who advocated my promotion, I believe that my promotion was a consolation prize for turning down my initial application for the senior role; they offered me the junior role instead, which I reluctantly accepted. However, after observing my work in the first few months, I believed they realized that I was capable to take on a senior role. With that said, I do believe there was a degree of tokensim involved; they now had someone to evidence the diversity of the senior leadership team. To avoid such misinterpretations, I should have requested that the senior leadership team explain to colleagues that I exceeded the job specification for a senior role and that the work that I produced in my first few months warranted reconsideration of my senior application.

> **Perspective 2:** Introduce the second party, describe their unique viewpoint and speculate why they held that viewpoint.

> **Narrator voice:** Explain what could have been done to rectify their misinterpretations.

The 'back and forth' consists of four simple steps

1. **Overview of issue:** Introduce the issue and indicate that the issue is not seen in the same way by you and another party.

    Example sentences:
    - *I worked on the proposal to implement a hybrid work model to enhance flexibility, but my supervisor was concerned that it would hinder team communication and collaboration.*

- *While I saw value in adopting a more casual dress code to create a relaxed work environment, the HR department believed it would negatively impact the company's professional image.*
- *I explained that investing in new firmware would improve our efficiency, but the finance team was hesitant because of the upfront costs and potential disruption during the transition.*
- *I advocated the shortening of meetings to increase productivity. In contrast, some team members felt that it would not allow enough time for thorough discussions, etc.*

2. **Perspective 1:** Describe your viewpoint and reasons for adopting this viewpoint.
3. **Perspective 2:** Introduce the opposing party, describe their counterview and reasons that support their counterview.
4. **Resolution:** State how the clash of viewpoints was resolved or the realization that was gained from clash.

Example of 'back and forth'

When I handed in my three months' notice to pursue a degree in Human Resources, I did not expect it to cause such friction with the director of the company. From my perspective, I had to consider my long-term aspirations and personal growth. Returning to university was a chance to deepen my knowledge, gain new skills, and ultimately prepare myself for future challenges and opportunities. I assume that the tension caused by my resignation was due to the Director's conception of the company as a 'family'. To him, I was not leaving a workplace, I was turning my back on the 'family'. Smith (2022) explains that there is a tendency of companies that uphold such conceptions to expect unconditional loyalty and make setting boundaries

Overview of issue: Introduce the issue and indicate that the issue is not seen in the same way by you and another party.

Perspective 1: Describe your viewpoint and reasons for adopting this viewpoint.

Perspective 2: Introduce the second party, describe their unique viewpoint and speculate why they held that viewpoint.

difficult. All of this resonated with me and typified my experience at the company. The tension made me realize that leaving wasn't just about moving on to something new; it was also about acknowledging the impact I had made and the void I would leave behind. Additionally, I realized I could have done more to communicate my intentions clearly and respectfully, before I handed in my resignation.

> **Resolution:** State realization that was gained from clash.

41 Uncovering power in your reflection

The last and most profound approach seeks to uncover power. Power is not always detectable. Thus, reflect on the ways that power has revealed itself to you within the context of the experiences or situations discussed. Revealing power deepens the reflective process. It moves beyond surface-level descriptions of events to a more nuanced analysis of the underlying factors that shape situations, decisions and behaviours.

There are two approaches to incorporating 'uncovering power' into your reflection

Approach 1: Uncovering a power grab

This approach seeks to uncover a 'power grab' in which someone subtly attempts to exert their authority over you or usurp your authority. It may appear to be just a conversation or a straightforward email, but if you dig deep enough, you will find a 'power grab'. Behind their seemingly innocuous words and actions is a well-thought-out strategy. This strategy doesn't have to be motivated by malevolence; they may seek to exert their authority over you or usurp your authority out of desperation, misinterpretation, insecurities or normalization.

Example of 'uncovering a power grab'

I invited a contractor into my office to talk about his drop in performance. During our conversation, I laid out plans to address the drop in performance; then he indicated subtly that he was senior to me in age. At first, I ignored it, then we carried on talking. After a while, he mentioned it again in a more explicit way. It seemed that he was trying to use his age to lessen my authority. I was perturbed by his

 This section of the paragraph is a surface-level description of an interaction.

 This section of the paragraph scratches beneath the surface to reveal what is *actually* happening. Notice the use of cautious words ('It seemed', 'he seemed' and 'I'm assuming'); this is because this is my interpretation of what happened, I cannot 100 per cent guarantee that it is correct, so caution is advised

interjection. Even though I had oversight over the project, he seemed to believe that his age outflanked my senior position; I'm assuming he resorted to using his age because he could not appeal to the company's hierarchical structure to exercise power. In response, I read the company policy on contractors; this acted as a shield to protect my authority. What was most interesting about this conversation was that so much was left unsaid; we did not mention 'power' or 'authority'; only after reflecting on the conversation, did I get a better idea of what we were *really* talking about.

> This section of the paragraph is the resolution. How was it resolved? What was the key takeaway?

Approach 2: Uncovering your different types of power

This approach seeks to uncover different types of power. On the surface, it may seem like just an interaction, or a simple command, but when you dig deeper, you realize the type of power being exerted. As Table 7.1 demonstrates, there are several types of power. You can select what is most relevant to your reflection.

Table 7.1 Types of Power (Stanley, Bennett and James, 2023)[4]

Type of power	Description
Reward power	This power is exercised by the ability to grant rewards or favours, such as, bonuses, time off or anything of value.
Coercive power	This type of power is derived from the capacity to generate fear. It may involve threats (real or implied) such as transfer, reassignment, demotion or dismissal.

[4]Stanley, D., Bennett, C. and James, A. (2023), *Clinical Leadership in Nursing and Healthcare*, Hoboken, NJ: Wiley-Blackwell, p. 387.

Legitimate power	This is the power of authority and commonly accompanies titled positions. It implies feelings of obligation or responsibility to concede to such powers.
Expert power	This power comes from knowledge, expertise or experience that others place value on. It is the embodiment of the phrase 'knowledge is power'. It is limited to a specialized area.
Referent power	This power is a type of influence that comes from being liked, admired or respected. People are drawn to this power or what it symbolizes. It can be paralleled with charismatic power.
Resource power	Controlling a variety of resources will imply a degree of power. This may be the control of budgets or staff promotion opportunities or anything that has a relative value or that may be scarce.
Informational power	This is derived from having access to selected or specialized information and knowledge or the means to control the access to the informational flow.

Example of 'uncovering your different types of power'

I noticed how my coworkers talked to the new director; it was deferential and almost passive. Their tone and attitude dramatically changed when conversing with her. Seemingly, the director role embodied legitimate power, which is the power of authority that commonly accompanies titled positions (Stanley, Bennett and James, 2023, p.387). People with legitimate power can influence others, demand compliance, and make decisions over others (Almond, 2019).

> This section of the paragraph is a surface-level description.

> This section of the paragraph scratches beneath the surface to reveal what is *actually* happening. Notice the use of a cautious word (Seemingly); this is because this is my interpretation of what happened, I cannot 100 per cent guarantee that it is correct, so caution is advised.

Part 8

How to write a dissertation

How to write a dissertation

This section will guide you through writing a dissertation, from beginning to end. A dissertation is a research project that is completed towards the end of your undergraduate or postgraduate degree; a dissertation is sometimes referred to as a project. Dissertations and projects are an opportunity to focus on a particular question or problem. It is the longest piece of academic work you will produce. Although you will have some support from an appointed supervisor, it is almost entirely independent.

Generally, a dissertation has five chapters. The templates will provide a guide for structuring your dissertation. In addition to structure, these templates will provide you with prompts to enhance the critical nature of your writing. Due to the diversity of dissertation content, this chapter will offer several options of templates to suit the needs of your dissertation.

This Part will provide you with templates for developing your research aim, abstract and each chapter of your dissertation.

42. How to develop a research aim

Research aim template 1: The 'traditional' aim

Research aim template 2: The 'problem/solution' aim

Research aim template 3: The 'case study' aim

Research aim template 4: The 'approach' aim

Research aim template 5: The 'sandwich' aim

43. How to write an introduction
Introduction template 1: The 'problem' approach
Introduction template 2: The 'gap' approach

44. How to write a literature review
Literature review template 1: The 'building' approach
Literature review template 2: The 'stitching' approach
Literature review template 3: The 'interview' approach

45. How to write a methodology
Methodology template 1: Primary research
Methodology template 2: Secondary research

46. How to write the findings/results and discussion/analysis chapters
Results and discussion template 1: Joint approach
Results and discussion template 2: Separated approach

47. How to write the conclusion chapter

48. How to write an abstract

Caution: if your lecturers have instructed you to follow a specific dissertation structure, you should follow that structure and only use this chapter to supplement your structure.

42 How to develop a research aim

This section will provide five templates to write a research aim for your dissertation.

Research aim template 1: The 'traditional' aim
Research aim template 2: The 'problem/solution' aim
Research aim template 3: The 'case study' aim
Research aim template 4: The 'approach' aim
Research aim template 5: The 'sandwich' aim

A research aim is a sentence that outlines the primary goal of your research. It encapsulates what you intend to achieve or investigate. The research aim is the foundation of your dissertation or project. A research aim needs to be clear, focused, achievable and relevant.

Does your research aim have to be completely original?

Do not worry if you have seen a similar research aim in a previous study because you can modify the details of your study to distinguish it from others. For example, even though you may have a similar aim to a previous study, you can set your research in a different time period, therein making your research unique. Likewise, you can use a different methodology, different data analysis approach, different geographical location, etc.

Types of research aims

There are five common approaches to developing your aim. These approaches are interrelated, so it is possible to merge or edit them to suit your needs.

Research aim template 1: The 'traditional' aim

The traditional aim comprises three features to form one sentence: (1) topic (2) area (3) target. This aim will suit most traditional dissertations. It starts very broad, then narrows with each part:

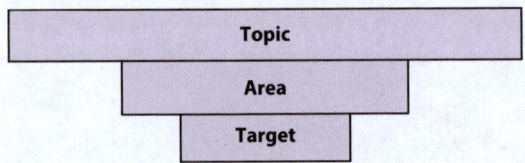

Topic: The first stage of constructing this aim is to consider which topic to research. A topic is a matter that you have studied in your degree, read in your reading list or discussed in your class; for example, well-being is a topic that is studied within the organizational psychology degree. So, which topic did you find the most captivating? It is not a requirement that you studied the topic intensely, only that it stood out to you; it interested you the most. Alternatively, which topic would be advantageous for your career? Many organizations would appreciate a dissertation on a topic that they were concerned about.

Area: After you have selected a topic, you need to focus on a specific area. This is because a topic alone is too broad, you need to focus on a specific sector or industry. For example, if you select the gender pay gap, this is too broad, so instead, you opt to focus on the gender pay gap in the advertising sector. Typical sectors are early years, higher education, further education, banking, advertising, automotive, construction, etc. Also, you may want focus even further than these broad examples; for example, instead of placing your research in the banking sector, you would like to focus even further on the Islamic banking sector.

Target: Within your selected area you should focus on a target population. A target population is a specific group of individuals or entities that you intend to study. This population is defined by certain characteristics. For example, your target population may be neurodivergent healthcare assistants, third-year students, female managers, lecturers from a South Asian background, etc. When you have selected your target population, you may want to focus on their experiences, knowledges, skills, motivations, choices, behaviours, challenges, strategies, circumstances, etc.

Example of the traditional aim

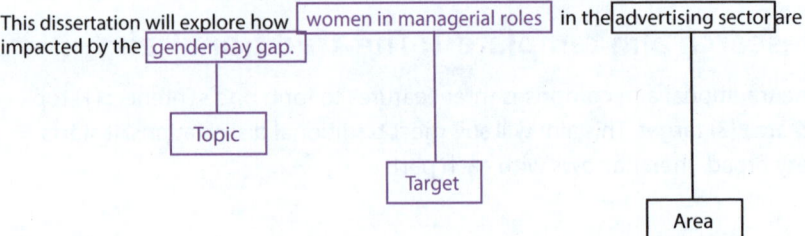

Research aim template 2: The 'problem/solution' aim

The second type of aim is the problem/solution aim, which is an aim that mentions a problem and the seeking of a solution. Your research is focused on finding out more about a problem in order to address, mitigate, lessen, redirect or solve it. This aim consists of two features: (1) problem (2) solution.

Problem: When selecting a problem to research, consider which problems were discussed in class or what you came across in the literature. Your problem must align with three matters. First, this problem should be something that exists in the real world; perhaps it has impacted you in your workplace, or it was something discussed in the media. Second, it is important that the problem that you choose to research must relate to one of the subjects that you studied in your degree. Third, it must be considered a problem by all parties; there should not be any doubt that it is a problem.

Solution: The 'solution' feature of the aim is just a general indication of the intent to work towards a solution. The solution in your aim will be vague because the solution will only become clear after thoroughly researching the problem. Additionally, some problems cannot be solved, so it may be that you are working towards a betterment, mitigation, lessening or redirection.

Examples of the problem/solution aim

This dissertation seeks to understand the motivations of **healthcare professional's refusal to participate in clinical trials** with a view to propose more effective ways of engagement.

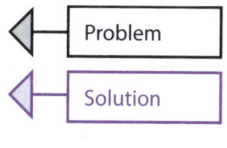

The purpose of this research is to assess the **challenges to international students achieving a good degree** in order to propose guidance to UK universities.

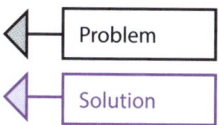

Research aim template 3: The 'case study' aim

The third approach of a research aim is a case study aim. This aim includes a case study to tell a wider story or to chart a wider development. The case study aim consists of three features: (1) case study (2) unique angle (3) wider issue (optional).

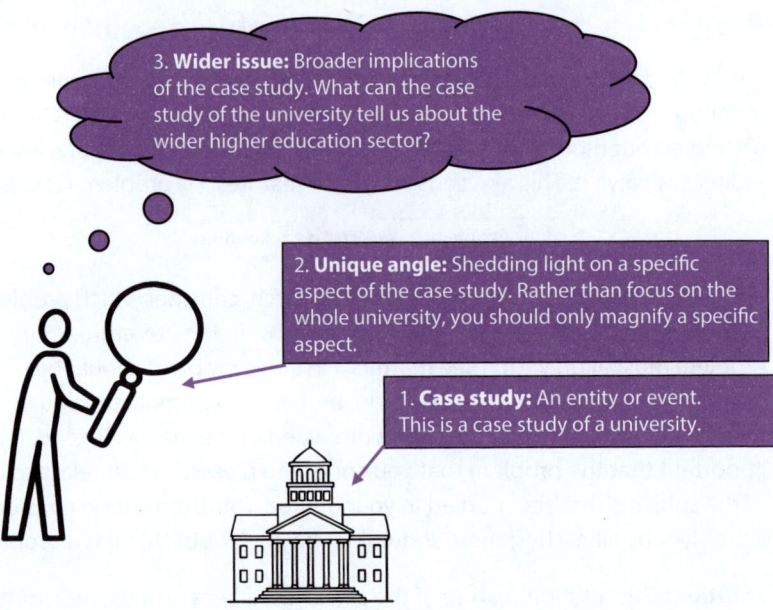

Case study: A case study approach is focusing on an entity or event. You focus on an entity or an event because it is a real-life example of a much wider issue. An issue may be too broad, so instead, you focus on a smaller unit like an entity or an event. For example, you may focus on the negotiations during the 2024/25 strike over staff pensions at a particular university in order to provide a typical real-life example of the wider issue of declining pensions in the higher education sector. Focusing on the 2024/25 strike over staff pensions at a particular university allows you to put forward a more detailed, nuanced and focused explanation. Examples of a case study are ChatGPT, Tesco, Brexit, 2024 UK race riots, Covid-19 lockdowns, Microsoft, etc. It is important that the case study is not a rarity; it must be a typical example of the broader point that you want to make.

Unique angle: The second feature is a unique angle; narrow your research by thinking about which angle or aspect you want to focus on. For example, ChatGPT is too broad to focus on, thus, your unique angle could be to look at how students engage with ChatGPT to complete assessments.

Wider issue (optional): The third feature is the wider issue. The wider issue does not have to be explicitly mentioned in your aim because it may make your aim too wordy or overly complicated. The wider issue is the broader implications of your case study research; what can your case study research tell us about wider issues? For example, a case study exploring remote working at a particular organization can tell us about the wider issue of the new era of work or the lasting impact and influence of the pandemic. It is important that the wider issue relates to the topics covered in your degree.

Examples of the case study aim

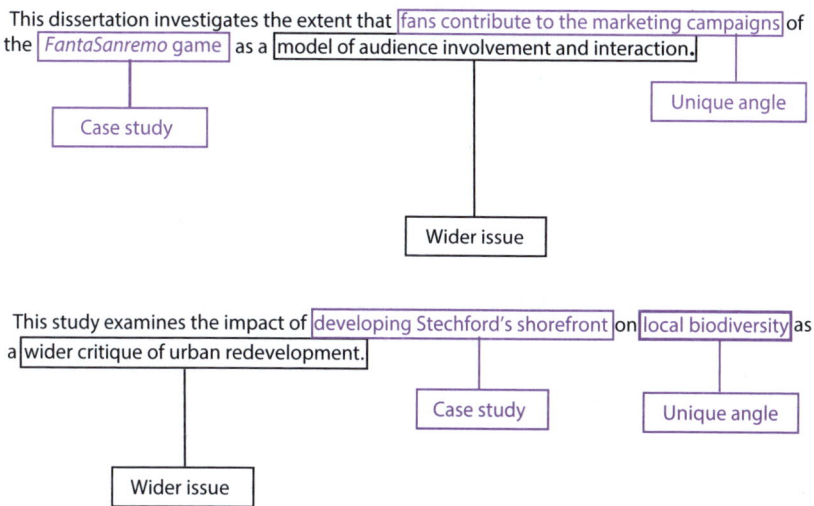

Research aim template 4: The 'approach' aim

The approach to your research is explicitly stated in the aim. This approach is that you research a specific matter using a specific theory, concept, model or framework. This aim consists of two features: (1) approach (2) activity, event or an entity.

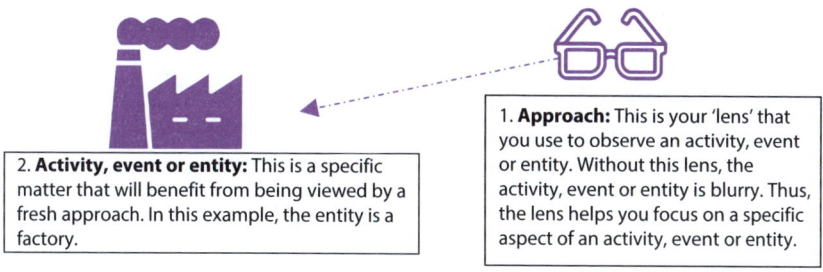

Approach: You should select an approach for your research; an approach is a specific theory, concept, model or framework that you have discussed in class or came across in your module reading list. Your approach acts as a lens to observe an activity, event or an entity. If you were to observe an activity, event or an entity without a lens, it may be too broad, messy or overly complex; a lens helps you home in on a specific aspect. For example, university staff recruitment is a broad activity, therefore, you opt to use a critical race theory approach to focus on racial disparities in the university recruitment process. Moreover, using an approach provides a structured way to analyse an activity, event or an entity; activities, events or entities can be understood in a systematic way. When you use an approach to your research, you do not have to use it in on every page of your dissertation and you are free to use other approaches. However, it must be the dominant approach of your dissertation that impacts your methodology and how you analyse your data. Additionally, you will need to justify your use of the approach at some point in your dissertation.

Activity, event or an entity: You need to think about which activity, event or an entity warrants the use of an approach; consider at least one of these questions when choosing an activity, event or an entity. Which activity, event or an entity will benefit from your use of an approach? Will new knowledge be produced from applying an approach to the activity, event or an entity? Can the activity, event or an entity be ameliorated or enhanced by using the approach? Additionally, try to make the activity, event or an entity specific. For example, 'policing' is too general, opt instead for 'stop and search procedures in Manchester, England'.

Example of the approach aim

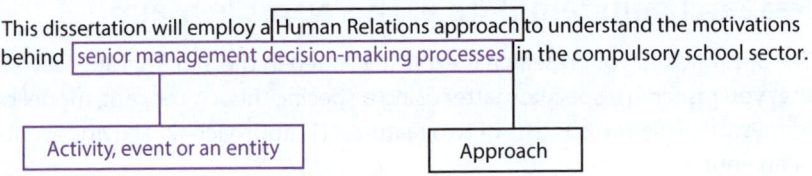

Research aim template 5: The 'sandwich' aim

This aim incorporates two separate topics and seeks to compare them or assess their relationship. This aim consists of three features: (1) topic (2) filling (3) topic.

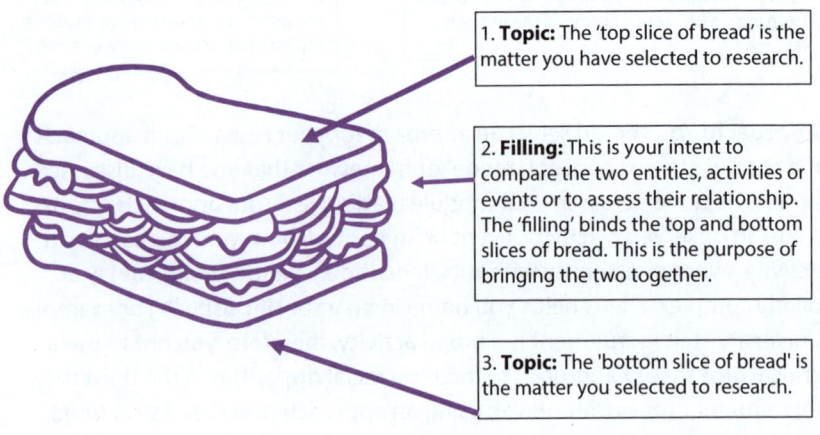

1. **Topic:** You mention a topic in your aim that you intend to research. The term topic is used very broadly; it can refer to an activity, event or an entity, it can even extend to a concept, theory, model or framework. Your topic can be fairly broad because if it is too specific, it may be too difficult to compare with another topic. The only boundary of this feature is that it should be related to something that you studied in your degree.

2. **Filling:** This feature is where you explain what you intend to do with both topics; you can compare and contrast them, assess their relationship, analyse how one topic leads to the other topic, examine how one topic impacts the other topic, etc.

3. **Topic:** You mention a second topic in your aim that you intend to research.

Example of the sandwich approach

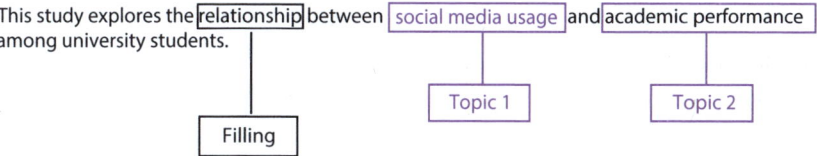

43 How to write an introduction

This section will provide you with two templates to write the introduction chapter of your dissertation/project. The introduction chapter of your dissertation is a crucial section that paves the way for your entire research project. The introduction chapter is designed to provide the reader with a clear understanding of what your dissertation is about and why it matters. Moreover, it highlights your research in a way that entices the reader to read the rest of the dissertation. All chapters are numbered using the decimal system. The major sections are 1.0, 2.0 or 3.0, and so forth, with subsection headings numbered as 2.1, 2.2, etc. This is a good method to follow.

There are two approaches to writing an introduction chapter:

Introduction template 1: The 'gap' approach

Introduction template 2: The 'problem' approach

Introduction template 1: The 'gap' approach

This template is for students who are seeking to 'fill' a gap in the academic literature. A gap is an area that has not yet been explored or is underexplored in the academic literature. There may be aspects of a topic that have not been examined yet. These gaps in knowledge might involve questions no one has tried to answer, perspectives no one has considered, or bodies of information that no one has attempted to collect or to analyse. A gap can be identified in two ways. First, you cannot find any or much literature on a specific matter even after you have consulted your university librarian. You cannot find literature on the representation of specific groups or types of organizations, lack of literature on the use of a particular method or approach to study a specific issue, insufficient literature with empirical data on a specific issue, lack of a theoretical or conceptual understanding of an activity that takes place in the real world, etc. Alternatively, you may have found that although there is sufficient literature, there remains a lack of practical application of theoretical knowledge in a specific real-world situation. Second, you have come a recent study that mentioned that there is a gap. Often studies will mention the gaps in their field.

What follows is a template of the 'gap' approach; it contains key sections and examples to write a captivating and engaging introduction chapter.

1.0 Introduction

In these opening paragraphs, you should:

- Provide a broad overview of your dissertation's topic area. This is a gentle introduction to the reader. For example, if your dissertation evaluates the impact of 3D printing on patient care, your broad overview may look like this: *Once used primarily for industrial manufacturing, three-dimensional printing techniques have become commonplace in various aspects of the healthcare industry.* If your dissertation assesses the impact of social media on mental health, your broad overview may look like this: *Social media has become integral to our daily routines: we interact with family members and friends, and join online communities. The amount of time people spend on social media has directed researchers' attention toward the potential benefits and risks.* If you are finding it difficult to write a broad overview, journal articles are great sources of inspiration. Most journal articles will begin with an overview; search for an article in the same subject area as your dissertation.

- State the aim of your dissertation in a sentence. Your aim should be a single sentence that describes the intent of your dissertation. This sentence should be straightforward and concise. For example: *This dissertation will evaluate the efficacy of mindfulness-based interventions in reducing stress among postgraduate students at the University of Warwick.*

    Examples:
    - This thesis investigates the way in which the …
    - This dissertation seeks to give explanation to the development of …
    - This dissertation seeks to examine the changing nature of …
    - The overall aim of this dissertation is to review the evidence for …
    - This dissertation applies Ubuntu methods to address …
    - This dissertation examines the emerging role of …
    - This dissertation systematically reviews the literature on …, aiming to provide …
    - This dissertation intends to determine the extent to which …
    - This dissertation aims to unravel some of the misconceptions surrounding …
    - Drawing upon two strands of research into …, this dissertation attempts to …

- Citing academic literature, briefly define the key terms of your dissertation aim. For example, if the aim of your dissertation is: *To assess the efficacy of occupational stress management programmes in the advertising sector*, then you would need to define 'occupational stress management programmes' and the 'advertising sector'. What do these words mean? What is the context behind these words?
- If possible, show the relationship between the key terms of your dissertation aim; what is the connection between 'occupational stress management programmes' and the 'advertising sector'? Provide a brief explanation of their interconnectedness. Alternatively, if the key terms are distinct from one another, provide a brief explanation of why they are not discussed together.

1.1 Background

- Provide a brief overview of the current level of knowledge – state what is currently known about your dissertation aim. Although you believe that there is a specific gap in knowledge, there must be some general knowledge around your aim. Therefore, this section acknowledges the existence of some knowledge.

  Examples:
  - *Studies over the past two decades have provided important information on …*
  - *The current state of research on … reveals insights into …*
  - *The current literature on … provides a general understanding of …*
  - *Existing research on … indicates that …*
  - *Existing research recognizes the critical role played by …*
  - *It is now well established from a variety of studies, that …*
  - *A growing body of published work provides evidence of …*

- Provide a brief overview of the gap; explain what has been unexplored or underexplored in the academic literature. Since this section contrasts with the above section, you must make it clear that despite the availability of general knowledge, this is still a significant gap.

  Examples:
  - *However, there is very little published research on …*
  - *However, it is still not known whether …*
  - *However, much less is known about …*
  - *However, the nature of remains unclear …*

- o   *However, what is less clear is the nature of …*
- o   *However, what is not yet clear is the impact of …*

All these examples start with 'however'; this is because, in the above section, you explained which knowledge is currently available. Therefore, in this section, you need to explain that the current knowledge is not acceptable. 'However' is a transitional word that shows contrast or conflict between two ideas.

- Postulate reasons why there is a gap. Why have scholars and experts not filled this gap? It may be due to the speed of social formations, legislation or world events, or technological advancement has outpaced scholarship; geographical bias; inherent challenges of accessing data (such as gathering company data on workplace bullying). When possible, substantiate your reasoning by citing academic literature. It is important that you use cautious language (e.g. arguably, possibly, may, seems) when postulating possible reasons for the knowledge gap because you may be right or wrong.

    Examples:
    - o   *The gap seems to be due to lack of methodological diversity in previous research.*
    - o   *The interdisciplinary nature of the topic appears to have contributed to the research gap.*
    - o   *Arguably, the knowledge gap exists because most studies have focused on Global North populations, leaving the experiences of individuals in the Global South underexplored.*
    - o   *The rapid expansion of ChatGPT appears to have outpaced pedagogical research.*

1.2 Rationale

- Justify the need to fill the gap. Since scholars and experts have not filled the gap, you will need to justify why you want to fill it. Explain why it is advantageous to fill the gap; is filling the gap beneficial to wider society? Is filling the gap helpful to the field? Is filling the gap an opportunity to hear previously unheard voices? Is filling the gap a way to move beyond an impasse?

    Examples:
    - o   *This is the first study to …*
    - o   *This work will generate fresh insights into …*

- It is anticipated that findings from the project will help guide …
- The present research explores, for the first time, the effects of …
- The findings should make an important contribution to the field of …
- This study aims to contribute to this growing area of research by exploring …

- Additionally, you can explain the ramifications if the gap remains unexplored/underexplored.

1.3 Research questions or aim and objectives

- In this section, state your **research questions**, or your **aim and objectives.** Choose whatever suits the needs of your dissertation and the requirements of your department. Your research questions are derived from your dissertation aim. Your research questions are specific, focused and relevant questions that will help you achieve your aim. Thus, your research questions are steps towards fulfilling your central dissertation aim. For example, if the aim of your dissertation is to explore the impact of social media in improving university students' academic performance, then crucial research questions to ask are:

1. *What is the relationship between social media and students' academic performance?*
2. *Which specific aspects of social media impact the learning of university students?*
3. *How does social media impact the academic performance of students compared to traditional classroom methods?*

- Alternatively, if you prefer, you can use aims and objectives instead. In a sentence, state the central aim of your dissertation and state two or three objectives. Like research questions, objectives are areas that you need to cover to reach your aim. For example, if your central aim is to travel to Birmingham, your objectives will be to pack your suitcase, travel to airport, etc.

Example:

Aim: *To analyse the impact of the coronavirus pandemic on the consumer use of fitness apps.*

Objective 1: *To assess the frequency of the consumer use of fitness apps pre- and post-pandemic.*

Objective 2: *To investigate the relationship between digital fitness and traditional forms of fitness (in-gym) in the aftermath of the pandemic.*

Objective 3: *To identify the factors driving the fitness apps following the pandemic.*

1.4 Overview of dissertation

Briefly describe each chapter of your dissertation. This is a generic example:

This dissertation will include a literature review of existing research relevant to the study. This will be followed by the methodology chapter, which details the research design and methods employed, explaining the rationale behind the chosen approaches and addressing ethical considerations. In the results chapter, the findings of the research are presented, with supporting data and key considerations. The discussion chapter interprets these results, offering insights into their significance and applicability. Finally, the conclusion chapter summarizes the key findings, reflects on their implications, and provides recommendations for future action and research.

Introduction template 2: The 'problem' approach

This template is for students who are seeking to address a problem. This is the most popular approach. A problem could be any of these four scenarios:

1. An area of concern.
2. Something to be improved upon.
3. A difficulty to be eliminated.
4. A contradiction that needs to be resolved.

1.0 Introduction

In these opening paragraphs, you should:

- Provide a broad overview of your dissertation's topic area. This is a gentle introduction to the reader. For example, if your dissertation evaluates the impact of 3D printing on patient care, your broad overview may look like this: *Once used primarily for industrial manufacturing, three-dimensional printing techniques have become commonplace in various aspects of the healthcare industry.* If your dissertation assesses the impact of social media on mental health, your broad overview may look like this: *Social media has become integral to our daily routines: we interact with family members and friends, and join online communities. The amount of time people spend on social media has directed researchers' attention towards the potential benefits and risks.* If you are finding it difficult to write a broad overview, journal articles are great sources of inspiration. Most journal articles will begin with a broad overview; search for an article in the same subject area as your dissertation.

- State the aim of your dissertation in a sentence. Your aim should be a single sentence that describes the intent of your dissertation. This sentence should be straightforward and concise. For example: *This dissertation will evaluate the efficacy of mindfulness-based interventions in reducing stress among postgraduate students at the University of Warwick.*

    Examples:
    - *This thesis investigates the way in which the …*
    - *This dissertation seeks to give explanation to the development of …*
    - *This dissertation seeks to examine the changing nature of …*
    - *The overall aim of this dissertation is to review the evidence for …*
    - *This dissertation applies Ubuntu methods to address …*
    - *This dissertation examines the emerging role of …*
    - *This dissertation systematically reviews the literature on …, aiming to provide …*
    - *This dissertation intends to determine the extent to which …*
    - *This dissertation aims to unravel some of the misconceptions surrounding …*
    - *Drawing upon two strands of research into …, this dissertation attempts to …*

- Citing academic literature, briefly define the key terms of your dissertation aim. For example, if the aim of your dissertation is: *To assess the efficacy of occupational stress management programmes in the advertising sector*, then you would need to define 'occupational stress management programmes' and the 'advertising sector'. What do these words mean? What is the context behind these words?

- If possible, show the relationship between the key terms of your dissertation aim; what is the connection between 'occupational stress management programmes' and the 'advertising sector'? Provide a brief explanation of their interconnectedness. Alternatively, if the key terms are distinct from one another, provide a brief explanation of why they are not discussed together.

1.1 Background

- Citing the academic literature, explicitly state what the problem or issue is.
- Explain why the problem is detrimental, unsafe, unproductive, unsustainable, untenable, inconsistent or contradictory. Often

a problem will be stated but it is not entirely clear why it is a problem. Thus, in this section, be very explicit, state why it is a problem.

- If relevant, who or what is impacted by the problem. A problem may not be a problem to all parties.
- If relevant, discuss the prevalence of the problem. Use statistics and/or scholarly commentary to show the prevalence of the problem.
- Citing the academic literature, postulate what led to the problem. Problems do not just happen, there are usually antecedents, prior signs or conditions/factors that gave rise to the problem. Do not delve too deep into history, just surmise relevant information, Also, it is important that you use cautious language (e.g. arguably, possibly, may, seems) when postulating possible reasons that led to the problem because you may be right or wrong.
- Describe what is currently being done to address the problem: What have scholars and/or practitioners put forward to address or ameliorate the problem? What has the government done through legislation, regulation, policy, etc., to address or ameliorate the problem? However, if the problem has not received attention from the government, scholars or practitioners, postulate why this is so.

1.2 Rationale

Explain why the problem needs to be addressed; is addressing the problem beneficial to wider society? Is addressing the problem helpful to the field? Is addressing the problem a way to move beyond an impasse?

Examples:

- *This is the first study to …*
- *This work will generate fresh insights into …*
- *It is anticipated that findings from the project will help guide …*
- *The present research explores, for the first time, the effects of …*
- *The findings should make an important contribution to the field of …*
- *This study aims to contribute to this growing area of research by exploring …*

Additionally, you can explain the ramifications if the problem is not addressed.

1.3 Research questions or aim and objectives

In this section, state your research questions, or your aim and objectives. Choose whatever suits the needs of your dissertation and the requirements of your department. Your research questions are derived from your dissertation aim. Your research questions are specific, focused and relevant questions that will help you achieve your aim. Thus, your research questions are steps towards fulfilling your central dissertation aim. For example, if the aim of your dissertation is to explore the impact of social media in improving university students' academic performance, then crucial research questions to ask are:

1. What is the relationship between social media and students' academic performance?
2. Which specific aspects of social media impact the learning of university students?
3. How does social media impact the academic performance of students compared to traditional classroom methods?

Alternatively, if you prefer, you can use aims and objectives instead. In a sentence, state the central aim of your dissertation and state two or three objectives. Like research questions, objectives are areas that you need to cover to reach your aim. For example, if your central aim is to travel to Birmingham, your objectives will be to pack your suitcase, travel to airport, etc.

Example:

Aim: To analyse the impact of the coronavirus pandemic on the consumer use of fitness apps.

Objective 1: To assess the frequency of the consumer use of fitness apps pre- and post-pandemic.

Objective 2: To investigate the relationship between digital fitness and traditional forms of fitness (in-gym) in the aftermath of the pandemic.

Objective 3: To identify the factors driving the fitness apps following the pandemic.

1.4 Overview of dissertation

Briefly describe each chapter of your dissertation. This is a generic example:

This dissertation will include a literature review of existing research relevant to the study. This will be followed by the methodology chapter, which details the research design and methods employed, explaining the rationale behind the chosen approaches and addressing ethical considerations. In the results chapter, the findings of the research are presented, with supporting data and key considerations. The discussion chapter interprets these results, offering insights into their significance and applicability. Finally, the conclusion chapter summarizes the key findings, reflects on their implications, and provides recommendations for future action and research.

44 How to write a literature review

This section will provide you with three templates to write the literature review chapter of your dissertation/project:

- Literature review template 1: The 'building' approach
- Literature review template 2: The 'stitching' approach
- Literature review template 3: The 'interview' approach

Before we discuss the templates, it is important to note that there are two types of literature reviews:

1. **The literature review empowers you to reach your research goal:** The first type of literature review prepares you for research by empowering you with the existing knowledge. Without such knowledge, it would be difficult to design your study, collect data and analyse the data. Moreover, you may end up doing the same study as someone else because you were not aware of the existing knowledge.

2. **A literature review is your research goal:** Essentially, the literature review is considered your research. The sole purpose of your research is to review the literature. In this type of literature review, the introduction chapter introduces the literature review, the methodology chapter designs the literature review, the results show the results of the literature review, the discussion discusses the literature review, and finally the conclusion and recommendations come out of the literature review.

The three templates used in this chapter are for the first type of literature review. For information on the second type of literature review, refer to page 171. Nonetheless, despite their differences, both types of literature reviews provide comprehensive summaries and analysis of existing research on a particular topic. Thus, you should avoid writing the literature in the style of the illustration below. This approach is merely a list of every publication that was read, publication by publication. There is no grouping or ordering of the literature; this reveals a lack of managing the literature.

Literature review

Introduction

Rajpal (2002) states …

Smith (2013) argues …

Singh (2017) explains …

Henry (2000) contends …

Conclusion

In contrast to the above example, the three templates enable you to impose conceptual order on the material you have read. Your imposition of order is what separates a good literature review from a poorly written one. Moreover, each template will help you situate your dissertation on top of what came before; this is an important aspect of literature reviews that is often absent. You are not compelled to follow every aspect of the four templates. If you wish you can add, omit or combine aspects.

You do not have to copy the headings or subheadings in any of the four templates, feel free to be creative and name your sections whatever is more relevant to you.

Literature review template 1: The 'building' approach

The first template is the building approach. This is the most popular approach. The essence of this approach is that you build upon what came before you; you construct a picture of the main publications that discuss your dissertation topic; not every single publication, just the main publications that were written before your dissertation. This is done to situate your dissertation on top of the main publications. Your dissertation is the latest instalment of what came before.

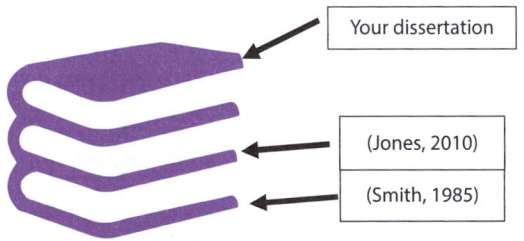

You can ascertain the main publications in a topic area by paying attention to the articles that are frequently cited by other researchers. These are often considered foundational or influential in the field. Also, in class, you often hear about the most important publications. Additionally, you can read the literature review chapter of a PhD thesis in a related field (see page 25), consult with your university librarian and refer to textbooks.

2.0 Introduction

The literature review should start with a small introduction. The introduction consists of two aspects:

- Explain the purpose of your literature review chapter.

  Example:
  - *The purpose of this chapter is to critically evaluate the body of literature in order to provide a foundation for this study.*

- Provide a brief overview of the areas that your literature review will cover.

  Example:
  - *This literature review will cover three areas. First, the historical development of ... Second, the key theoretical frameworks that have shaped ... Finally, there will be a discussion on how this dissertation builds upon what came before.*

2.1 Overview of the literature

- Provide an overview of the main ideas in your dissertation topic area. If possible, provide the overview in chronological order. Do not discuss every single text, pick out the standout texts that have impacted your dissertation. You should see yourself as an editor, not a reporter.

  Examples:
  - *Wenger's study is of great significance as it marks the first attempt to assess the broader impact of ...*
  - *The first detailed study of ... was conducted by ...*
  - *Henry's 2017 study was among the first to examine ...*
  - *Before Arthur's groundbreaking study (1978), it was generally believed that ...*
  - *One of the most cited studies is Bergkamp and Henry's (2010) study who saw ...*
  - *Seaman's studies in the 1970s helped to establish an explanatory model for ...*

- ... is most commonly associated with the work of Sterling (1980).
- Arguably the best-known study using this approach was carried out by Saliba (2017).

Like an editor, you should group similar texts together in different categories (see page 76 for tips).

Examples:
- *There are four general approaches currently being adopted in the literature. One is ...*
- *The existing literature can be broadly categorized into three main themes. First, ...*
- *The literature can be approached from multiple perspectives ...*
- *It is possible to identify two broad themes in the literature ...*
- *The works of Brazant fall under three headings: (1) ..., (2) ..., (3) ...*

Also, similar to an editor, you should divide this section into subheadings of the various areas that you cover. For example:

2.1.1 Initial studies on utilizing artificial intelligence in selection and assessment

2.1.2 Theories on utilizing artificial intelligence in selection and assessment

2.1.3 Emerging issues of utilizing artificial intelligence in selection and assessment

- If possible, mention contextual factors that impacted or shaped the literature. For example, if your focus was on female workers in the IT industry and you noticed that there was a sudden influx of studies on remote work's impact on female workers in the IT industry from the 2020s, you can attribute this to the Covid-19 lockdowns. Equally, the literature can have been impacted or shaped by the expansion of artificial intelligence technologies, public opinion, growth of STEM initiatives to attract recruitment from underrepresented groups, etc.

2.2 Limitations of the literature

In relation to your dissertation's specific area of focus, state the limitations that you found in the literature. This section is important because it legitimizes your dissertation and clears the path for your dissertation to sit on top of what came before. By showing the limitations in the literature, you are indirectly providing a rationale for your dissertation. If there were no limitations, then there would be no need for your dissertation. Therefore, in this section, state the limitations, criticisms, problems and gaps of the literature. This is carried out in two steps:

- **The first step:** You zoom in to state the limitations, criticisms, problems and gaps of individual publications within your dissertation's topic area. To find out how to criticize publications, refer to the section on criticizing academic texts, page 75–88, and finding critical information, page 18.

    Examples:
    o Bernado's study (2021) suffers from …
    o Saka (2011) fails to specify …
    o Hart (2013) makes no attempt to …
    o The scope of Young's study (2005) was relatively narrow, being primarily concerned with …
    o The key problem with Lennon's explanation is that …
    o However, there is an inconsistency with French's main argument
    o One of the limitations with this explanation is that it does not explain why …

- **The second step:** You zoom out to critique the entire body of literature; imagine that all the individual publications that touch on similar topics are one body, then you launch a general critique against this entire body. This is a skill of a critical thinker that you can treat individual publications as part of one body of literature. Your critique of this body of literature focuses on its limitations and missed opportunities. This creates a space for your dissertation to fill.

    Examples:
    o Overall, these studies reveal the lack of attention given to …
    o Together, these studies indicate that …
    o Two significant limitations emerge from the studies discussed so far. First, …
    o However, this body of literature remain narrow in focus, dealing only with …
    o All the studies reviewed here have failed to engage with …
    o In view of all that has been mentioned so far, we can identify two striking issues with the literature. First, …

2.3 Building on the literature

In this section, you will situate your dissertation as a successor to the existing literature. In relation to the limitations that you discussed in the above section, suggest how your dissertation will enhance the body of literature. You can suggest that you are enhancing literature by taking the literature in a different direction, or by expanding or narrowing the focus, etc.

2.4 Conclusion

- Summarize the main points of the chapter.

  Examples:
  - *This literature review points to the following general conclusions regarding …*
  - *This chapter provided a summary of the literature relating to …*
  - *In summary, it has been shown from this review that …*
  - *From the studies reviewed here, it is evident that …*
  - *To conclude this section, the literature identifies …*
- Escort the reader to the next chapter.

  Example sentences:
  - *Having identified the key themes and gaps in the existing literature, the next chapter will detail the research methodology designed to address these gaps and contribute new insights to the field.*
  - *The insights gained from the literature review inform the methodological choices discussed in the following chapter.*
  - *The critical issues and opportunities highlighted in the literature review set the stage for the methodological approach described in the next chapter.*

Literature review template 2: The 'stitching' approach

The second template is the stitching approach. The essence of this approach is stitching two or more topic areas together. You are bringing them together because they are rarely found in the literature together, so you are the one that must do the stitching. The two or more topics that you have selected are generally discussed individually, but not together. For example, you may want to research the impact of remote working on neurodiverse workers, so you found that there are numerous articles on neurodiverse workers and numerous articles on remote work, but there were not any articles that discuss both neurodiverse workers and remote work, so you must stitch these two topics together.

2.0 Introduction

The literature review should start with a small introduction. The introduction consists of two aspects:

- Explain the purpose of your literature review chapter.

    Example:
    - *The purpose of this chapter is to combine insights from the fields of neurodiversity and remote work in order to develop a more holistic understanding of how neurodiverse workers are impacted by remote work.*

- Provide a brief overview of the areas that your literature review will cover.

    Example:
    - *This literature review will provide an overview of the literature on remote work and the neurodiverse workforce. The latter half of the literature review will seek to bring both strands of literature together.*

2.1 Topic area (the heading for this section is the name of one of your topic areas)

Provide an overview of one of your topic areas.

Examples:
- *The following discussion provides an overview of …*
- *This section will provide an overview of the key concepts and theories in the topic of …*
- *Recently, considerable literature has grown up around the topic of …*
- *This overview will examine the development of …*

2.2 Bridging the gap

This is where the stitching takes place; justify the need to stitch another topic area onto the topic area that you discussed in 2.1. You can mention that the literature in the topic area that you discussed in 2.1 is too limited, too narrow, too outdated or lacking in depth, so it needs to be complemented with another topic area. How does the integration of two topics offer a new or deeper perspective? Essentially, this section clears the path to introduce the second topic area in 2.3.

2.3 Topic area (the heading for this section is the name of one of your topic areas)

Provide an overview of one of your topic areas.

> Examples:
> - *The following discussion provides an overview of …*
> - *This section will provide an overview of the key concepts and theories in the topic of …*
> - *Recently, considerable literature has grown up around the topic of …*
> - *This overview will examine the development of …*

2.4 Fusion of literature

In 2.2, you only provided the justification for bringing two topics together, therefore, in this section, you need to provide a detailed description of what the fusion looks like. You are attempting to show a finished product of two or more topics fused together. After you describe the fusion, here are some possible questions to think about. What has been achieved through this fusion? What are some themes or ideas that emerge from this fusion? What are the expectations of the fusion? How does the fusion benefit your research objectives or research questions? What is a possible tension or conflict with this fusion and how will you overcome it? How does this fusion prompt further research?

If possible, you can also provide a graphical representation or model of the fusion for further clarity.

2.5 Conclusion

- Summarize the main points of the chapter.

  Examples:
  - *This literature review points to the following general conclusions regarding …*
  - *This chapter provided a summary of the literature relating to …*
  - *In summary, it has been shown from this review that …*
  - *From the studies reviewed here, it is evident that …*
  - *To conclude this section, the literature identifies …*

- Escort the reader to the next chapter

Example sentences:
- ○ *Having identified the key themes and gaps in the existing literature, the next chapter will detail the research methodology designed to address these gaps and contribute new insights to the field.*
- ○ *The insights gained from the literature review inform the methodological choices discussed in the following chapter.*
- ○ *The critical issues and opportunities highlighted in the literature review set the stage for the methodological approach described in the next chapter.*

Literature review template 3: The 'interrogation' approach

The third template is the 'interrogation' approach. The essence of this approach is to interrogate the suitability of a theory, model, framework or concept to use in your research. This approach is for those committed to using a single theory, model, framework or concept to analyse an activity, event or entity. For example, your dissertation will utilize the concept of 'cultural fit' to analyse the selection and assessment practices of advertising agencies in the UK. Therefore, your literature review will 'interrogate' the concept of cultural fit to assess if it is suitable for its intended purpose.

2.0 Introduction

The literature review should start with a small introduction. The introduction consists of two aspects:

- Explain the purpose of your literature review chapter.

  Example: *The purpose of this chapter is to interrogate the suitability of critical race theory to analyse the recruitment practices of UK investment banks.*

- Provide a brief overview of the areas that your literature review will cover.

  Example: *This literature review will commence with an overview of the literature on the recruitment practices of UK investment banks. This is followed by an interrogation of critical race theory as a tool to analyse recruitment practices of UK investment banks. The last section will detail the modifications made to the critical race theory lens to enhance its suitability.*

2.1 Overview of literature on … (the name of the activity, event or entity)

In this section, provide an overview of the literature on the activity, event or entity that you are researching. For example, if you are using the human-centred approach to look at government structures in Peru, then in this section, you will document the literature on government structures in Peru. Or if you are using the concept of digital sustainability to assess UK startups in the tech industry, then in this section, you will document the literature on UK startups in the tech industry.

After the above overview of the activity, event or entity, you will need to point out the shortcomings of the literature on the activity, event or entity. This is done to justify your use of a concept, theory, model or framework. Your use of a concept, theory, model or framework must be predicated on an enhancement or rectification of the existing literature. If the existing literature doesn't need to be enhanced or rectified, then your use of a concept, theory, model or framework has no justification. Thus, it is imperative to point out the shortcomings of the literature on the activity, event or entity. This creates a space for your dissertation to offer a new perspective.

Examples:
- *Overall, these studies reveal the lack of attention given to …*
- *Together, these studies indicate that …*
- *Two significant limitations emerge from the studies discussed so far. First, …*
- *However, this body of literature remains narrow in focus, dealing only with …*
- *All the studies reviewed here have failed to engage with …*
- *In view of all that has been mentioned so far, we can identify two striking issues with the literature. First, …*

2.2 Overview of … (the concept, theory, model or framework)

Provide an overview of the concept, theory, model or framework.

2.3 The usefulness of … (the concept, theory, model or framework)

State the potential benefits, advantages or justification of using the concept, theory, model or framework to analyse the activity, event or entity.

This establishes your rationale for using the concept, theory, model or framework.

Examples:
- *This theory provides valuable insights into …*
- *Overall, this concept offers a powerful explanation of …*
- *This framework is particularly helpful owing to its focus on …*
- *The model provides us with a useful lens to view …*

2.4 Studies that utilized the … (the concept, theory, model or framework)

Discuss a study or studies that utilized the concept, theory, model or framework to observe an event, activity or entity. If possible, try to find studies within the same topic area as your dissertation. It is important to review past studies to situate your research amongst them and to show that your use of the concept, theory, model or framework is not out of ordinary, you are following the tradition of other scholars. It is also an opportunity to demonstrate critical thinking by assessing how studies used the concept, theory, model or framework: were the other studies use of the concept, theory, model or framework adequate or inadequate? What did the authors say about their use of the concept, theory, model or framework?

Examples:
- *This study builds on previous uses of stewardship to observes the choices made by senior leadership teams.*
- *Similar to this dissertation, Al-Ubaid's research also employed a critical race theory lens to explore the relationship between …*
- *There are three studies that utilized postcolonial theory to observe higher education institutions, however, they did not share this dissertation's focus on assessment practices.*
- *Mensah's work is grounded in academic literacies, the same theory underpinning this research, and it demonstrates how …*
- *This study builds on previous uses of stewardship to observes the choices made by senior leadership teams.*

2.5 The limitations of … (the concept, theory, model or framework)

State the potential disadvantages/criticisms of using the concept, theory, model or framework to analyse the activity, event or entity. Whenever you engage with models, frameworks, theories and concepts, it is important to critique them. This is because models, frameworks, theories and concepts are a simplification of the real world, they are mainly accurate, but they are not the real world. Therefore, there will be some degree of misalignment with the real world. This section requires very light critique; do not be overly critical about the concept, theory, model or framework because, if you are too negative, the marker will be confused as to why you selected the concept, theory, model or framework. However, if there is a major criticism, suggest ways to mitigate it. For tips on critiquing models, frameworks, theories and concepts, refer to pages 73–85 and to find criticisms of models, frameworks, theories and concepts, refer to page 18.

Examples:

- *There are limits to how far the model can be taken.*
- *There are two issues with using critical race theory in the context of investment banking. First, …*
- *Critics question the ability of the framework to provide …*
- *The main limitation with this model is …*
- *One criticism of much of the literature on … is that …*

2.6 Adaptation of … (the concept, theory, model or framework)

Building on the above-mentioned limitations, you will need to adapt the concept, theory, model or framework to suit the specific circumstances of your research. This is just a slight modification of the concept, theory, model or framework to better suit the needs of your dissertation. For example, you may have come across a model that has five stages, but only four are relevant for your dissertation, therefore, you will just use four and explain why. The concept may need to be updated, reduced, extended or complemented with another concept; whatever the case, adapt it and provide a rationale for your adaptation.

Examples:

- *In line with the above-mentioned limitations, the theory has been adapted to better explain the motivations of …*
- *Given the unique context of this dissertation, the framework has been adapted to incorporate three additional factors. First, …*
- *While it provides a strong foundation, the framework has been modified to account for the dissertation's UK focus.*

- Recognizing the limitations of the concept in its original form, two aspects have been modified to more effectively explore the experiences of … First, …

Emphasize how your adapted concept, theory, model or framework is a fresh and unprecedented approach.

Examples:
- By modifying the original concept, this research opens new avenues for understanding … that challenges traditional views on …
- This modified framework marks a slight departure from its conventional usage, providing an unprecedented lens through which to examine …
- By integrating elements not previously considered, the framework offers an original contribution to the literature, paving the way for further research into …
- The adjustments made to the existing concept resulted in a fresh approach to the study of …

2.7 Conclusion

- Summarize the main points of the chapter.

    Examples:
    - This literature review points to the following general conclusions regarding …
    - This chapter provided a summary of the literature relating to …
    - In summary, it has been shown from this review that …
    - From the studies reviewed here, it is evident that …
    - To conclude this section, the literature identifies …

- Escort the reader to the next chapter.

    Example sentences:
    - Having identified the key themes and gaps in the existing literature, the next chapter will detail the research methodology designed to address these gaps and contribute new insights to the field.
    - The insights gained from the literature review inform the methodological choices discussed in the following chapter.
    - The critical issues and opportunities highlighted in the literature review set the stage for the methodological approach described in the next chapter.

45 How to write a methodology

This section will provide two templates for writing a methodology:

Methodology template 1: Primary research

Methodology template 2: Secondary research

The methodology is usually the second or third chapter of a dissertation. Essentially, a methodology consists of explaining how you designed your research project and justifying the choices you made. Methodologies should be written in the past tense because you are explaining what you have already done. Also, you can strengthen your explanations and justifications by citing this book, research textbooks, and literature from your subject area.

Methodology template 1: Primary research

When should you use this primary research methodology template?

This template is for you if you are gathering original data that has not been collected before. This data can include interviews, surveys, observations or any type of research that you go out and collect yourself.

3.0 Introduction

In your opening paragraph:

- State the aim of the methodology chapter. Try to avoid a generic aim; link the aim to the details of your research.

    Example:

    ○ *This chapter will provide the methodological approach used to collect and faithfully analyse the experiences of young men in the construction industry.*

- Briefly explain how your methodology is arranged.

    Example:

    ○ *This chapter outlines the research design, including the data collection methods and the sampling approach used to select participants. It also details the procedures for data analysis and discusses the steps taken to ensure ethical considerations were met. It concludes with a discussion on the limitations of the research methods.*

3.1 Research paradigm

In this section, you should outline your research paradigm. A research paradigm is a systematic way of observing one's reality. Thus, your chosen research paradigm will influence whether the study is qualitative or quantitative. The most common research paradigms that students choose from are positivist/post-positivist (quantitative), interpretivist (qualitative), critical realist (qualitative and quantitative), constructivist (qualitative), and critical theory (qualitative). Choose the paradigm that will suit the focus of your study. A benefit of choosing a research paradigm is that it helps you avoid lengthy, complex and detailed discussions on research philosophy (ontology and epistemology) because research paradigms contain a specific ontology and epistemology. In a sense, research paradigms come pre-packaged, the work is already done. By stating your research paradigm, you have also stated your ontological and epistemological positioning.

Caution: Only some subjects require you to explain your research paradigm; if you have been given no explicit instruction to describe your research paradigm, consult your supervisor.

- Citing literature, define the research paradigm that you selected.

    Example:

    - *This study adopted the critical realist approach (CR). CR is a philosophical system developed by … CR assumes that events in our world can be understood only if people understand the structures that generate these events.*

- Justify your research paradigm; put forward reason(s) for selecting this paradigm. Your justification may be that the paradigm aligns with your research objectives.

    Example:

    - *CR was selected because it was best suited to making sense of the complexity of business relationships and networks in the UK advertising industry.*

Your justification could be that the paradigm aligns with your views as a researcher; one's views about epistemology, which means the nature of knowledge, can influence the choice of paradigm. For example, a researcher who believes that knowledge is constructed through our social interactions may adopt a social constructivist research paradigm, whereas an individual who believes in a detached objective reality may lean towards the post-positivism research paradigm.

Example:

- *A social constructivist paradigm was adopted due to the view that knowledge is co-constructed through interactions within specific contexts.*

Your justification can also relate to your preferred mode of data collection. For example, your research is designed to incorporate qualitative data collection methods because you want to conduct an in-depth exploration of attitudes; in this case, your research is best suited to the interpretivist research paradigm. Alternatively, your research is designed to incorporate quantitative data collection methods because you want to analyse numerical data; in this case, your research is best suited to the positivist paradigm.

Example:

- *The interpretivist paradigm was selected to facilitate the use of qualitative methods, which are essential for understanding the lived experiences of the research participants.*

Your justification can be to remain consistent and comparable with the literature in the field. After your literature review, you found that the vast majority of studies utilized a particular research paradigm; thus, to situate your research amongst the existing research, you opted to adopt the same research paradigm.

Example:

- *Following the established research tradition in this field, a critical theory paradigm was chosen to critically analyse social inequalities.*

3.2 Research design

- In this section, you should state whether your approach was qualitative, quantitative or based on mixed methods. Qualitative research is an exploratory approach that aims to understand occurrences in real-life settings. It often involves gathering non-numerical data, such as interviews, observations and focus groups. Qualitative research is particularly useful for exploring complex social phenomena, attitudes and behaviours. In contrast, quantitative research is a systematic investigation of observable and apparent occurrences through statistical, mathematical or computational techniques. Mixed methods research combines elements of both qualitative and quantitative research. After stating your chosen approach, you should offer a very brief definition derived from academic sources.

- Justify your qualitative, quantitative or mixed methods approach

    Example:

    ○ *This research adopted a mixed-method approach to look at the attainment gap that exists between students in a post-1992 university … This approach aided the research aim by gaining a more comprehensive understanding of the award gap through the collection and analysis of both numerical and non-numerical data. The goal was to provide a more complete and nuanced view of the award gap.*

- Additionally, in this section, you should state whether your approach was deductive or inductive: deductive research involves testing a theory or hypothesis by collecting and analysing data. Deductive reasoning is often associated with quantitative research methods, where researchers aim to confirm or disconfirm existing theories or hypotheses. Inductive research is a bottom-up approach where the researcher begins with specific details and observations and then works towards developing broader generalizations or theories. It can also involve the search for patterns from observations of occurrences and then developing 'theories' to explain what was observed. Inductive research is often associated with qualitative research methods. After stating your chosen approach, you should offer a very brief definition derived from academic sources.

- Justify your deductive or inductive approach.

    Examples:

    ○ *An inductive approach was adopted due to the exploratory nature of the research, which seeks to …*

    ○ *Given the qualitative nature of the study, an inductive approach was appropriate as it allows for the emergence of themes and patterns directly drawn from the interview data.*

    ○ *The deductive approach was justified by the quantitative nature of the study.*

    ○ *A deductive approach was adopted because the dissertation aims to test existing theories in …*

    ○ *Given the objective of this research is to test a pre-defined hypothesis, a deductive approach was deemed appropriate.*

3.3 Participants

- Describe your participants. A research participant is an individual who takes part in a research study or experiment. These participants are the individuals from whom researchers observe or collect data in order to address specific research questions, test hypotheses or explore phenomena of interest.

    Example:
    - *Eight female project managers from the higher education sector aged between 30 and 60 from Greater London, UK were selected to explore the impact of the gender pay gap on female professionals.*

- State which sampling approach you used to obtain the participants of your study. Additionally, define your chosen sampling approach. A sampling approach refers to the process of selecting individuals or elements/organizations to participate in your study.

    There are several sampling approaches, each with its own advantages and limitations:
    - Random sampling: Participants are chosen from a population either by using a random number table or a random number generator. Each member of the population has an equal, independent and known chance of being selected.
    - Convenience sampling or consecutive sampling: Participants who are readily available and represent the phenomenon of interest are included in the sample.
    - Snowball sampling: Participants who are known to and recommended by current participants are identified and included, building the sample from a few participants to as many as are needed.
    - Purposive sampling: Participants are intentionally selected because they have certain characteristics that are related to the purpose of the research.

    Example:
    - *Participants were selected through snowball sampling, which is based on a referral approach (Arthur, 2024). I arranged to interview four female project managers who referred four of their colleagues who worked in similar organizations.*

- Justify the size of your sample and justify why you selected the approach.

Example:

- The small sample size of five project managers enabled the study to gather intricate and nuanced data. Snowball sampling was selected because it opened up the insulated social system of female project managers.

• State a limitation or a hurdle with your chosen sampling approach and how it was remedied or moderated.

Example:

- There was one limitation of using the snowball approach; the quality of referrals had the potential to be affected by a lack of diversity, as the female project managers were likely to refer others who were like themselves. This can result in a lack of diversity in the sample, making it difficult to generalize the findings to a broader population. This limitation was remedied by intentionally selecting the initial four female project managers from diverse backgrounds. Thus, the snowballing process was able to capture a wider range of perspectives, reducing the risk of homogeneity and increasing the representativeness of the sample.

3.4 Methods

• State and define your method(s) of data collection. Methodology refers to the overarching framework or strategy that guides the entire research process. Whereas method relates to the specific technique or procedure used to gather data, such as interviews, surveys, focus groups, questionnaires, etc.

Example:

- This study utilized semi-structured interviews. A semi-structured interview is a method of research in which the questions are loosely structured, which gives interviewees more opportunities to fully express themselves (King, 2022).

• Justify why you selected the method(s).

Example:

- Semi-structured interviews were selected to gain in-depth insights into marketing executives' perspectives, as it encouraged open dialogue and allowed the participants to express themselves in their own words.

• Explain how have you applied the method(s).

Example:

- The semi-structured interviews were conducted using Microsoft Teams at a time that was convenient for the participants. I went through my list of questions, but also allowed for flexibility. I let the conversation flow naturally, adapting based on the participant's responses. To supplement the recording, I jotted down key points, observations and non-verbal cues.

- State a limitation or a hurdle with the application of the method(s) and ow it was remedied or moderated.

    Example:

    ○ Contrary to face-to-face interviews, conducting interviews on Microsoft Teams limits the ability to observe participants' full body language and subtle non-verbal cues (Jackson, 2021). Therefore, close attention was paid to non-verbal cues, tone of voice, and pauses. Additionally, the participants were asked follow-up questions to explore any unclear or ambiguous statements, ensuring that the participant's meaning was faithfully interpreted.

3.5 Data analysis

- Explain how you analysed your data.

    Example:

    ○ This study drew out the key themes of the interview data using thematic analysis (TA). TA looks for connections within data, and identifies thematic patterns (Li, 2015). More specifically, this dissertation adopted Naeem et al.'s six step approach:[1] Step one: the researcher edited the interview transcripts in order to gain familiarity. This involved not only correcting errors but also selecting certain parts of the interview and leaving out others in order to make the transcript more concise and easier to analyse. Step two: …

- Justify why you selected this type of analysis.

    Example:

    ○ The selection of TA stems from two reasons. First, TA places a strong emphasis on the perspectives of participants, allowing their voices to be central in the interpretation of the data (Kent, 2020). Second, the process of TA ultimately results in a conceptual model that encapsulates the researcher's findings (Gant, 2025).

---

[1] Naeem, M., Ozuem, W., Howell, K. and Ranfagni, S. (2023), 'A Step-by-Step Process of Thematic Analysis to Develop a Conceptual Model in Qualitative Research', *International Journal of Qualitative Methods*, 22. https://doi.org/10.1177/16094069231205789; Byrne, D. (2022), 'A Worked Example of Braun and Clarke's Approach to Reflexive Thematic Analysis', *Quality and Quantity*, 56: 1391–1412. https://doi.org/10.1007/s11135-021-01182-y

- State a limitation or a hurdle with this analysis approach and how it was remedied or moderated.

    Example:
    - TA is vulnerable to researchers letting their own preconceptions interfere with the identification of key themes (John, 2022). This was moderated by maintaining a 'goal-free' evaluation that aligns with purpose of inductive research where theories are developed from the data (Scriven, 1991).

3.6 Ethical considerations

In one paragraph:
- Explain how you informed the participants what will happen with the research.
- Explain how you protected the participants' confidential/sensitive data.
- Explain how you anonymized the participants' confidential/sensitive data.
- Explain how you obtained consent from the participants.
- Explain that you gave the option for participants to withdraw their input.
- If available, indicate the case number of your ethical approval application.

3.7 Conclusion

- Summarize the chapter.

    Examples:
    - In conclusion, the methodology detailed in this chapter has provided a framework for investigating …
    - In summary, this chapter has detailed the methodological approach employed in this study, including the research design, data collection methods and analytical techniques.
    - In summary, through careful selection of the appropriate research methods, data collection techniques, analysis tools and ethical process, this study rests on rigorous, reliable and principled foundations.

- Take the reader to the next chapter.

    Example sentences:
    - With the methodology established, what follows is the Results chapter, where the data collected will be presented and analysed.

- The following chapter will present the findings derived from the methods discussed, offering a detailed account of the data collected and the patterns observed.
- As the dissertation transitions to the next chapter, the focus will shift from how the research was conducted to what the research has revealed.

Methodology template 2: Secondary research

When should you use this literature review template?

This template is for you if you are conducting secondary research. This means that your dissertation is restricted to the collection, analysis and synthesis of information that has already been published. Your dissertation does not include collecting new and original data directly from experiments, surveys, interviews, focus groups or observations.

3.0 Introduction

In your opening paragraph:

- State the aim of the methodology chapter. Try to avoid a generic aim; link the aim to the details of your research.

    Example:
    - This chapter outlines the methodological approach used to identify, evaluate and synthesize existing research studies on …

- Briefly explain how your methodology is arranged.

    Example:
    - This chapter will commence with a discussion on research questions that guide the review. This is followed by a detailed look at the search strategy, which is carefully outlined to ensure reproducibility. Then the criteria for the inclusion and exclusion of studies are clearly defined, ensuring that the selected literature is relevant and of high quality. The latter part of the chapter describes the process of data extraction and synthesis, which allows for the identification of key themes, trends and gaps in the existing research.

3.1 Objectives of the literature search

In this section, you state the objectives of the literature search. The objectives of your literature search are derived from your research question(s) or research objectives. For example:

Research questions	Literature search objectives
What is the relationship between social media and students' academic performance?	To assess the relationship between social media and students' academic performance?
Which specific aspects of social media impact the learning of university students?	To identify which aspects of social media impact the learning of university students.
How does social media impact the academic performance of students compared to traditional classroom methods?	To compare the impact of social media and traditional classroom methods on the academic performance of students.

3.2 Databases

In this section, state which database you used to search for information and provide a rationale for your choice of database. A database is a portal of

Database	Rationale
Google Scholar	Google Scholar was a good starting point for exploratory searches due to its wide reach. However, its results required further verification.
JSTOR	JSTOR was crucial for the historical focus of the dissertation because it offered valuable historical research, and it contained older literature that was not available in other databases.
Sociological Abstracts	This was selected because it provides abstracts and indexing of the world's sociology literature.

academic and expert literature. These databases are crucial tools for finding and accessing literature relevant to your topic. They allow you to search for literature efficiently by offering features like advanced search filters, citation tracking and access to full-text materials. If you are not sure which database to use, consult with your department or university librarian. Below is an example of stating the database and providing a rationale.

3.3 Search terms

In this section, you will need to reveal your search terms. Search terms in a literature search strategy are the specific words or phrases that you type into a database to retrieve relevant literature on a given topic. Search terms are crucial for identifying articles, books, reports and other academic sources that align with your research question. Well-chosen search terms can significantly improve the efficiency and effectiveness of your search. Your search terms are derived from the words in your research question(s) or research objectives. Extract the keywords/main terms from your research question(s) or research objectives; these keywords/main terms are your search terms. Reveal your search terms in a normal paragraph, table, concept map or chart.

Here is an example of a table:

Research questions	Search terms	Synonyms of search terms	Search string (Refer to page 15 for a discussion on the meaning of **OR / AND**)
Research question 1: What is the impact of 3D printing on healthcare in the UK?	3D printing, UK, healthcare	Three-dimensional printing, Additive manufacturing, Patient care, Health, Medical, Medicine, United Kingdom, Great Britain	3D printing **OR** three-dimensional printing **OR** additive manufacturing **AND** healthcare **OR** patient care **OR** medical **OR** medicine **AND** UK **OR** United Kingdom **OR** Great Britain

3.4 Inclusion and exclusion criteria

You will need to state your inclusion and exclusion criteria, which are the specific conditions or parameters used to determine which literature are considered relevant and which are irrelevant to your dissertation. These criteria help to focus your research and ensure the selection of appropriate sources or data.

Here is an example of a dissertation on the in-person and remote experiences of international students studying in the UK through Covid-19 lockdowns:

Inclusion criteria	Exclusion criteria
International students studying in a UK HEI	International students undertaking a distance learning degree
Peer-reviewed journal articles and books	Opinion pieces, editorials or non-peer-reviewed articles
Sources written in English	Duplicate records
Articles that are accessible in full text	
Studies from 2019 to 2025	

Examples:
- Publications were only included in the analysis if …
- To identify … the following parameters were used:
- Criteria for selecting the participants were as follows:
- A number of criteria were considered when selecting …

3.5 Selection process

In this section, you described how you dealt with the results of your search. More specifically, you can explain a simple three-step selection process:

Simple example

1. **Initial screening:** Fifty titles and abstracts were reviewed for relevance based on the inclusion and exclusion criteria.
2. **Full-text review:** The thirty articles that passed the initial screening were read in full to ascertain if they were relevant to the research questions.

3. **Final selection**: Twenty-seven articles met all criteria and were included in the literature review.

Alternatively, you can detail a more comprehensive three-step selection process using a specific tool. There are a variety of tools to systematize your selection process. The example below is the CASP tool:[2]

Comprehensive example

1. **Initial screening:** Fifty titles and abstracts were reviewed for relevance and appropriateness based on the inclusion/exclusion criteria.

2. **Full-text review:** From the full review, thirty articles were selected. To conduct a full review of the articles, this study utilized the Critical Appraisal Skills Programme (CASP). CASP enables you to systematically assess the trustworthiness, relevance and results of published journal articles. CASP was selected because it offers a clear framework with specific questions that guide researchers through a systematic assessment of published articles, ensuring no crucial aspect is overlooked. The CASP tool has ten questions for each article that you selected.

    I. Does the publication have a clear statement of the aims of the research?
    II. Does the publication have a qualitative methodology appropriate?
    III. Does the publication have a research design appropriate to address the aims of the research?
    IV. Does the publication have recruitment strategy appropriate to the aims of the research?
    V. Does the publication have data collected in a way that addressed the research issue?
    VI. Does the publication adequality consider the relationship between researcher and participants?
    VII. Have the publication's ethical issues been taken into consideration?
    VIII. Was the publication's data analysis sufficiently rigorous?
    IX. Does the publication have a clear statement of findings?
    X. How valuable is the publication to research?

[2]Long, H., French, D. and Brooks, J. (2020), 'Optimising the Value of the Critical Appraisal Skills Programme (CASP) Tool for Quality Appraisal in Qualitative Evidence Synthesis', *Research Methods in Medicine & Health Sciences*, 1(1): 31–42. doi:10.1177/2632084320947559

However, there was a limitation of the CASP tool; it is focused on the quality of the article, but not the relevance to the study's research question or context. Therefore, this study mitigated this limitation by supplementing the CASP tool with considerations of how well the study corresponded with the research question.

3. **Final selection**: Twenty-seven articles met all criteria and were included in the literature review.

To add more clarity to your selection process, you can include a diagram:

Example of a literature search strategy diagram

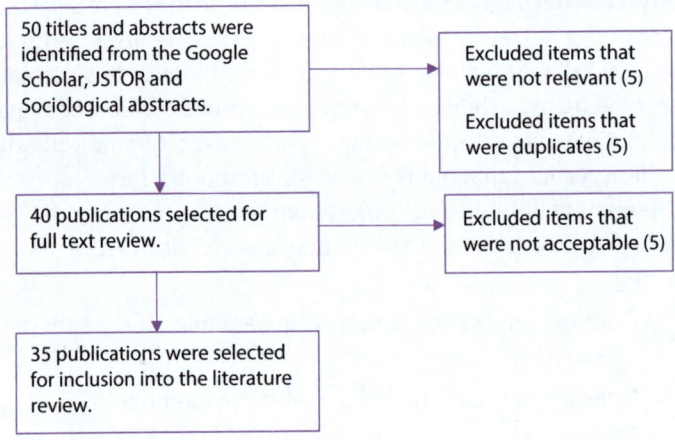

3.6 Limitations of the search strategy

Detail the limitations of your search strategy and how you addressed these limitations. For example, you can explain that a limitation of your literature search strategy was its exclusion of studies that were not written in English; this could have resulted in language bias and the exclusion of potentially relevant international studies. Then explain a way to mitigate this; you could mention that you utilized translation tools and professional networks to assess abstracts. Also, during your full review of each article, reference lists were examined to identify studies that may have escaped you, therefore, it is unlikely that a non-English study would have been missed if it was pivotal to the field.

Another possible limitation for you to explain is that the databases that you used may have had an incomplete coverage of the literature. In response, you can mention that this limitation was offset by your combination of multiple databases and using comprehensive databases like Google Scholar. Additionally, you could state that you undertook manual searches to supplement database limitations, ensuring a more comprehensive review.

Examples:

- The limitation of this search strategy is that …
- A disadvantage of this search strategy is that …
- The principal limitation of the search strategy is that …
- However, there are certain drawbacks associated with this search strategy …
- The disadvantage of this search strategy is its reliance on the availability of …

3.7 Ethical considerations

Although a literature review requires significantly less ethical considerations then studies that involve live subjects, it still requires adherence to ethical standards that ensure transparency, fairness and academic integrity.

- Bias: Explain that you mitigated bias by revealing limitations, using systematic appraisal tools and/or pre-defined criteria.
- Transparency: Explain that you maintained transparency by conducting a literature search that was clearly explained for others to replicate or understand the decisions made.
- Fairness: Explain that you represented the information from the included studies fairly and impartially. The data from included studies was not misrepresented or fabricated to align with a desired narrative.
- Proper attribution: Explain that the work of other researchers was used with proper attribution; proper citation was used to document the ideas, data and findings from studies.

3.8 Conclusion

- Summarize the chapter.

    Examples:

    - In conclusion, the methodology detailed in this chapter has provided a framework for investigating …
    - In summary, this chapter has detailed the methodological approach employed in this study, including the research design, data collection methods and analytical techniques.
    - In summary, through careful selection of the appropriate research methods, data collection techniques, analysis tools and ethical process, this study rests on rigorous, reliable and principled foundations.

- Take the reader to the next chapter.

  Example sentences:
  - *With the methodology established, what follows is the Results chapter, where the data collected will be presented and analysed.*
  - *The following chapter will present the findings derived from the methods discussed, offering a detailed account of the data collected and the patterns observed.*
  - *As the dissertation transitions to the next chapter, the focus will shift from how the research was conducted to what the research has revealed.*

46 How to write the findings/results and discussion/analysis chapter

The Findings chapter is used interchangeably with the Results chapter. The Findings/Results chapter of a dissertation is where you present your research findings. The Discussion chapter is used interchangeably with the Analysis chapter. The Discussion/Analysis chapter is where you interpret your research findings. There are two templates to writing the Findings/Results and Discussion/Analysis chapters:

Template 1: The Findings/Results chapter and Discussion/Analysis chapter are separated into two chapters.

Template 2: The Findings/Results chapter and Discussion/Analysis chapter are merged into one chapter.

Before we discuss the two templates, you first need to understand the relationship between Findings/Results and Discussion/Analysis sections. The Findings/Results and Discussion/Analysis chapters are 'sisters'. Although they have different purposes, they are intimately linked. The primary goal of the Findings/Results chapter is to *describe* your findings. In contrast, the primary goal of the Discussion/Analysis section is to *analyse* your findings.

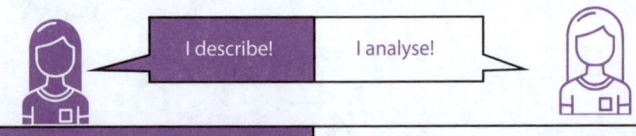

'Sister' 1: Findings/Results	'Sister' 2: Discussion/Analysis
Findings/Results chapter Describe your findings	Discussion/Analysis Analyse
Describing: The Findings/Results chapter requires you to describe your findings; this means that you simply present what you found, no analysis or interpretation is needed, just present what is apparent. For example, you may present the comments of your interviewees, but you will not critique, analyse or interpret the comments just present them to the reader. Nothing more than a surface-level observation is needed; it is not disputable, contentious or debatable. Additionally, when you describe, you should only state specific information about your findings. This means that you should zoom in on your findings; only present what you found, you should not try to 'zoom out' and connect your findings with the wider literature. You should only concern yourself with presenting your data. Do not look beyond your data; leave this to the Discussion/Analysis chapter.	**Analysing:** The Discussion/Analysis chapter requires you to analyse your findings; this means that you should provide the reader with more than just the surface meaning. Your collected data (statistics, comments, response, etc.) are essentially meaningless and contextless, so you need to interpret the data to uncover a deeper meaning. The original Greek meaning of 'analysis' is to set free. In this spirit, you need to 'set free' the deeper meaning from the words, responses or actions that you presented in the Findings/Results chapter. Additionally, analysis requires you to 'zoom out' and connect your findings with the wider literature; how does your data relate to or impact wider society? You show the value of your research by connecting specific details of your findings to the wider world.
Typically found in the Findings/Results section	Typically found in the Discussion/Analysis section
No significant differences were found between shoppers.	*The lack of differences found between shoppers can be attributed to several factors. First, the standardization of retail practices plays a significant role …*

There are two templates for writing the Findings/Results and Discussion/Analysis chapters.

Template 1: The Findings/Results chapter and Discussion/Analysis chapter are separated in two chapters.	Template 2: The Findings/Results chapter and Discussion/Analysis chapter are merged into one chapter.
This template is for those that want to separate the Findings/Results and Discussion/Analysis into two separate sections or chapters. You will present your findings in the Findings/Results chapter and in the following Discussion/Analysis chapter, you will analyse your findings. Therefore, you are talking about a similar topic/theme in two ways; descriptively in the Findings/Results chapter and analytically in the Discussion/Analysis chapter.	This template is for those that want to combine the Findings/Results and Discussion/Analysis into one chapter. You will present your findings in a paragraph(s), then in the following paragraph(s), you will analyse your findings. Therefore, you are talking about a similar topic/theme in two ways; descriptively in the first paragraphs and analytically in the following paragraphs.

Template 1: The Findings/Results chapter and Discussion/Analysis chapter are separated in two chapters

The Findings/Results chapter

In this chapter, you will describe your findings. Although you should avoid analysis, you can help the reader appreciate what you are presenting to them by emphasizing certain issues.

4.0 Introduction

- State the aim of this chapter.

    Example:

    - *This chapter presents the key findings of the research on postgraduate international students.*

- Explain how this chapter is arranged.

    Example:

    - *This chapter is organized around the research objectives outlined in the introduction chapter. Each section will address each objective, offering insights into the data collected. The chapter commences with a discussion on the frequency of the consumer use of fitness apps. The second section investigates the relationship between digital fitness and traditional forms of fitness (in-gym) in the aftermath of the pandemic. Finally, the chapter examines the factors driving the fitness apps following the pandemic, while identifying potential implications for both theory and practice.*

4.1 The heading of this section is derived from your research objective or research question

For example, if your research question is: *What is the role of ethics in the development of cloud-based typing assistants?* then your heading could be: *4.1 The role of ethics in the development of cloud-based typing assistant.* Alternatively, if your research objective is: *to identify the challenges of cultural awareness in coaching.* Then your heading could be: *4.1 the challenges of cultural awareness in coaching.*

Here is an example of transforming the research question or research objective into a heading:

Your research question	A heading of this chapter
What is the function of personal data in the development of cloud-based typing assistants?	4.1 The function of personal data in the development of cloud-based typing assistants
Your research objective	**A heading of this chapter**
To identify the challenges of cultural awareness in coaching	4.1 the challenges of cultural awareness in coaching

Present the findings from your surveys, interviews, questionnaires, focus groups, etc.

To accentuate your description of the data, you can use quotes, paraphrases, narration, graphs, tables, charts, etc.

Examples:

- *No significant differences were found between …*
- *The overall response to this question was very positive.*
- *The most interesting aspect of this graph is …*
- *What stands out in the table is …*

- What is striking about the figures in this table is …
- There was a significant positive correlation between …
- Opinions differed as to whether …
- Of interest here is the increase in …
- Another reported problem was …
- As one interviewee put it:

4.2 The heading of this section is derived from your research objective or research question

For example, if your research question is: *What is the role of ethics in the development of cloud-based typing assistants?* Then your heading could be: *4.2 The role of ethics in the development of cloud-based typing assistant.* Alternatively, if your research objective is: *To identify the challenges of cultural awareness in coaching.* Then your heading could be: *4.2 The challenges of cultural awareness in coaching.*

- Present the findings from your surveys, interviews, questionnaires, focus groups, etc.

    To accentuate your description of the data, you can use quotes, paraphrases, narration, graphs, tables, charts, etc. Make sure that the findings in this section align with the heading of this section.

    Examples:
    - *No significant differences were found between …*
    - *The overall response to this question was very positive.*
    - *The most interesting aspect of this graph is …*
    - *What stands out in the table is …*
    - *What is striking about the figures in this table is …*
    - *There was a significant positive correlation between …*
    - *Opinions differed as to whether …*
    - *Of interest here is the increase in …*
    - *Another reported problem was …*
    - *As one interviewee put it:*

4.3 The heading of this section is derived from your research objective or research question

For example, if your research question is: *What is the role of ethics in the development of cloud-based typing assistants?* then your heading could be:

4.3 The role of ethics in the development of cloud-based typing assistant. Alternatively, if your research objective is: *To identify the challenges of cultural awareness in coaching*, then your heading could be: *4.3 The challenges of cultural awareness in coaching.*

Present the findings from your surveys, interviews, questionnaires, focus groups, etc.

To accentuate your description of the data, you can use quotes, paraphrases, narration, graphs, tables, charts, etc. Make sure that the findings in this section align with the heading of this section.

Examples:

- *No significant differences were found between …*
- *The overall response to this question was very positive.*
- *The most interesting aspect of this graph is …*
- *What stands out in the table is …*
- *What is striking about the figures in this table is …*
- *There was a significant positive correlation between …*
- *Opinions differed as to whether …*
- *Of interest here is the increase in …*
- *Another reported problem was …*
- *As one interviewee put it:*

4.4 Conclusion

- Summarize the key themes of this chapter.

    Example:

    - *The findings from the survey highlighted three important developments of remote work; redefinition of work/life balance, downsizing office spaces and increased use of digital collaboration tools. These findings offer new insights into expansion of remote work in the UK.*

- Escort the reader to the Discussion/Analysis chapter.

    Example:

    - *While these initial findings provide a comprehensive overview of the data collected, they also raise important questions that will be addressed in the Discussion chapter.*

The Discussion/Analysis chapter

In the Discussion/Analysis chapter, you will analyse the findings you presented in the previous Findings/Results chapter. The Discussion/Analysis chapter and Findings/Results chapter are twin sisters; the headings will be similar and generally follow the same order. For example:

Chapter 4: Findings	**Chapter 5: Discussion**
4.0 Introduction	5.0 Introduction
4.1 Redefinition of work/life balance	5.1 Reasons for the <u>redefinition of work/life balance</u>
4.2 Downsizing office spaces	5.2 The impact of <u>downsizing office spaces</u>
4.3 Increased use of digital collaboration tools	5.3 The implications of <u>increased use of digital collaboration tools</u>
4.4 Conclusion	5.4 Conclusion

In the above example, there are three important points. First, Chapter 5's headings are an analytical version of Chapter 4's headings. This signals to the marker that Chapter 4 is taking a descriptive approach and Chapter 5 is taking an analytical approach. Second, although the Findings/Results chapter and Discussion/Analysis chapter have similar headings, it is important that you do not repeat yourself. Third, as demonstrated by the example, the Discussion/Analysis chapter is larger than the Findings/Results chapter. This is because the Discussion/Analysis chapter synthesizes your analysis, data and relevant literature. Most markers focus on the Discussion/Analysis chapter because it is the climax of your research; everything comes together in this section.

In this chapter, you will need to demonstrate your analytical abilities. Before we show the chapter template, it is important to review common analytical approaches that you should use in the Discussion/Analysis chapter.

Analysing statements

An effective analytical approach is to analyse statements. If your study includes statements from your research participants, you can analyse them to find a deeper understanding of their words. You can elaborate on their words to 'release' their true meaning. Often the most important things are left unsaid. For example, if an interviewee stated that, 'There are only two real universities in England.' You can elaborate on the classism and elitism of their words: *The phrase suggests that Cambridge and Oxford are the only 'real' or 'true' universities in terms of their reputation, academic excellence and social status, overshadowing other educational institutions.* From just a few words, you can write a paragraph about their true meaning. It is important to be cautious in language and conservative in interpretation. If possible, cite the literature to substantiate your interpretation of their words, in the above example, you cite the literature on elitist views towards Cambridge and Oxford.

Conflict

A common analytical approach is to show contradiction, conflict or tension in your findings and seek to resolve it. There are several aspects of conflict that can be analysed. The first aspect of conflict is when your findings contradict the literature; you need to highlight the contradiction and suggest why there is a contradiction. For example, you come across Freire's banking theory of teaching that posits the negative effects of 'depositing' information into students, but in your study, the students who had been subjected to this form of teaching did not exhibit any of the negative effects, in fact, their confidence and autonomy grew from this form of teaching. You will need to explain why your findings contradict the theory; what did the scholar overlook? Which variable muted his theory, and why? Were the scholar's ideas an oversimplification? Has something changed from when the scholar first made this statement? Another example is that you interview nurses in the NHS expecting to hear about 'burnout'; a common feature in the literature is prevalence of burnout amongst nurses. However, the nurses did not mention anything in relation to burnout. Therefore, you should highlight this omission and provide an explanation as to why this is so. Another example is:

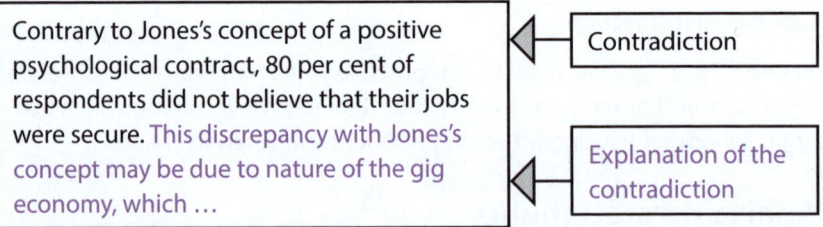

Another aspect of conflict is significant differences between the responses of your participants/respondents; this requires an explanation, especially if you did not expect such divergence. For example, you interview participant A, they make a statement, then you interview participant B, and they say the opposite. The lack of unity between responses signifies a problem because such difference means that you are unable to get a clear picture of what is happening; you are unable to see a pattern of behaviour; everything is chaotic. Such disarray requires an explanation. For example:

The participants expressed varying perspectives on the impact of remote work on their productivity. Their differing views on remote work productivity may have stemmed from their unique personal circumstances and home arrangements. For those with suitable home arrangements, they may have benefited more from remote working duties.	←	Differing perspectives
	←	Explanation of the differing perspectives You can substantiate your explanations by citing relevant literature, for instance, you can cite literature that mentions the importance of access to quiet, dedicated workspaces at home to get the most out of remote working.

Agreement

If you find that there is significant agreement between the responses of participants/respondents, their similar responses require an explanation. Although your participants/respondents may have been selected because of their similar backgrounds, their backgrounds are not identical; they are all individuals with differing life experiences. Thus, you will need to provide a possible explanation for the root cause of their consensus.

For example:

The respondents shared a remarkably consistent opinions on ethical considerations. This appears to be due to their ICF memberships; this may have informed their approach to coaching.	←	Consensus
	←	Explanation of the differing perspectives You can substantiate your explanations by citing relevant literature; for instance, regarding the above example, you can cite literature that mention the role of the accreditation process in encouraging shared professional values.

Prevalence

This is where you generalize a behaviour, process, act or occurrence identified in your findings. Rather than view the behaviour, process, act or occurrence as an isolated incident, you relate it to a wider prevalence. For example, in your findings, you noted that an older person felt that the healthcare staff had a pessimistic attitude towards her because of her age. Then you connect this specific occurrence with the literature on ageism:

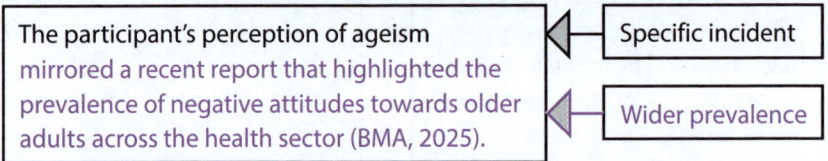

You can also demonstrate the wider prevalence through statistics:

You can evidence that what you observed in your study is not in line with the wider prevalence:

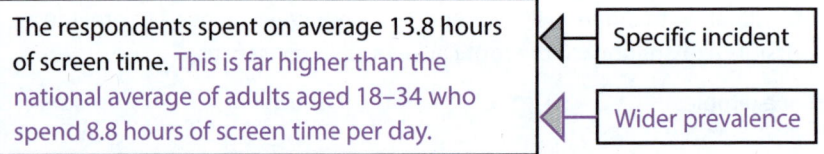

Wider context

You can contextualize your findings to give the reader a deeper understanding. By showing the wider context or wider reasons behind your findings, you have demonstrated that you have read widely. Moreover, explaining the wider context shows that you have considered the broader implications and complexities of your findings, not just the data itself. You can provide the context to several matters such as a statement from a respondent or you observed an activity or an interaction, etc; what is the context that gave rise to this occurrence? Perhaps it was a consequence of the wider organizational culture, or a recent relaxation of regulatory control. Here is an example of how context envelops much of what we observe:

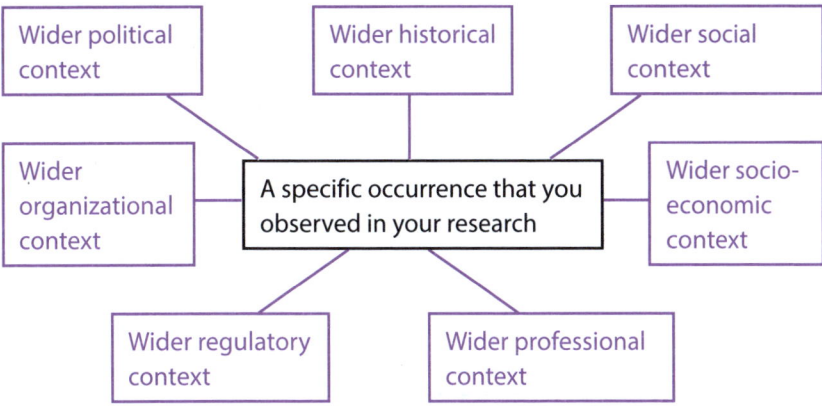

When providing the wider context, it is important to be conservative; the context needs to be plausible. Also, substantiate the wider context by citing the literature. For example:

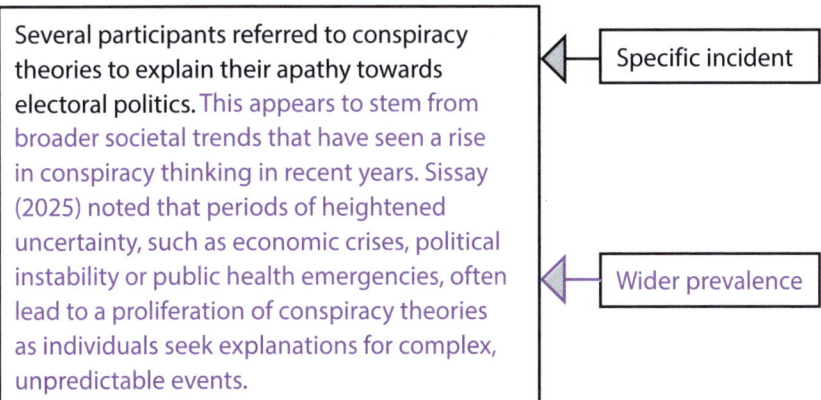

Conceptualization, using theories, concepts, models and frameworks

You should reinterpret what you observed using a concept, theory, model or framework. This will give the meaning. For example:

As discussed in the case study, Arthurcorp grew rapidly over a three-year period to offer a multitude of products. Girard (2023) refers to this as the 'Swiss army knife approach' to product development in which each of Google's products is simple to use and functions independently, but they are housed together and complement each other like a Swiss army knife.	← Details from your findings
	← This is a conceptualization to give the reader a deeper meaning. It is important that your conceptualization is drawn from academic literature.
Participant 1B's recounting of how their sales team formed was remarkably similar to Tuckman's (1999) theory of group development, which outlines five key stages: forming, storming, norming, performing, and adjourning. During the forming stage …	← Details from your findings
	← This is a conceptualization to give the reader a deeper meaning. It is important that your conceptualization is drawn from academic literature.

5.0 Discussion introduction

- State the aim of this chapter.

    Example:

    ○ *This chapter analyses the key findings of the research on postgraduate international students.*

- Explain how this chapter is arranged.

    Example:

    ○ *This chapter is organized around the research objectives outlined in the introduction chapter. Each section will address each objective, offering insights into the data collected. The chapter commences with a discussion on the frequency of the consumer use of fitness apps. The second section investigates the relationship between digital fitness and traditional forms of fitness (in-gym) in the aftermath of the pandemic. Finally, the chapter examines the factors driving the fitness apps following the pandemic, while identifying potential implications for both theory and practice.*

5.1 The heading of this section is similar to your heading of 4.1 in the previous Findings/Results chapter

For example, if your heading of 4.1 in the previous Findings/Results chapter is: *Downsizing office spaces*, then the heading of 5.1 can be: *The implications of downsizing office spaces*. This slight change in headings indicates to the marker that you are taking an analytical approach to the downsizing of office spaces. Additionally, for the sake of clarity, you can dissect your analysis into further sections, for example: *5.1.1 Practical implications of downsizing office spaces; 5.1.2 Conflicts of downsizing office spaces*, etc.

- This section should offer an analytical version of the descriptive account you presented in the previous Findings/Results chapter. You can use one or two of the approaches detailed on pages 187–192 to analyse your findings (analysing statements, conflict, agreement, prevalence, wider context or conceptualization).

  Examples:
  - *A possible explanation for this might be that …*
  - *This result may be explained by the fact that …*
  - *Several factors could explain this occurrence. First, …*
  - *These differences can be explained in part by …*
  - *This inconsistency may be due to …*
  - *The reason for this is not clear but it may have something to do with …*
  - *Unfortunately, these findings are rather difficult to interpret because …*

5.2 The heading of this section is similar to your heading of 4.2 in the previous Findings/Results chapter

For example, if your heading of 4.2 in the previous Findings/Results chapter is: *Downsizing office spaces*, then the heading of 5.2 can be: *The implications of downsizing office spaces*. This slight change in headings indicates to the marker that you are taking an analytical approach to the downsizing of office spaces. Additionally, for the sake of clarity, you can dissect your analysis into further sections, for example: *5.2.1 Practical implications of downsizing office spaces; 5.2.2 Conflicts of downsizing office spaces*, etc.

- This section should offer an analytical version of the descriptive account you presented in the previous Findings/Results chapter. You can use one of the approaches on page 185–190 to analyse your findings (analysing statements, conflict, agreement, prevalence, wider context or conceptualization).

Examples:
- A possible explanation for this might be that …
- This result may be explained by the fact that …
- Several factors could explain this occurrence. First, …
- These differences can be explained in part by …
- This inconsistency may be due to …
- The reason for this is not clear but it may have something to do with …
- Unfortunately, these findings are rather difficult to interpret because …

5.3 The heading of this section is similar to your heading of 4.3 in the previous Findings/Results chapter

For example, if your heading of 4.3 in the previous Findings/Results chapter is: *Downsizing office spaces*, then the heading of 5.3 can be: *The implications of downsizing office spaces*. This slight change in headings indicates to the marker that you are taking an analytical approach to the downsizing office spaces. Additionally, for the sake of clarity, you can dissect your analysis into further sections, for example: *5.3.1 Practical implications of downsizing office spaces; 5.3.2 Conflicts of downsizing office spaces*, etc.

- This section should offer an analytical version of the descriptive account you presented in the previous Findings/Results chapter. You can use one or two of the approaches detailed on pages 187–192 to analyse your findings (analysing statements, conflict, agreement, prevalence, wider context or conceptualization).

Examples:
- A possible explanation for this might be that …
- This result may be explained by the fact that …
- Several factors could explain this occurrence. First, …
- These differences can be explained in part by …
- This inconsistency may be due to …
- The reason for this is not clear but it may have something to do with …
- Unfortunately, these findings are rather difficult to interpret because …

5.4 The path forward

This section seeks to offer a solution, model, articulate a new vision, convey a new direction, or reimagine an issue. You are at a unique vantage point; you have read the relevant literature, collected data and analysed it. This places you in the best position to make an informed offering; this section symbolizes your unique contribution to existing knowledge. This section may involve describing a framework of engagement, model of practice, model of institution, model of behaviour, mode of praxis, code of practice, etc. You do not have to create a path forward completely from scratch, you can repurpose or adapt something that is already in existence.

- Articulate the need for a path forward. You will need to make explicit that the data you collected indicated a need for an intervention or rethinking. For example, the neurodivergent students that you interviewed spoke about their frustrations of having to disclose their diagnoses to lecturers for reasonable adjustments to made. This would happen every time they changed modules. Therefore, as a path forward, you describe a two-way secure digital platform where students can upload their diagnosis, necessary accommodations and comments. This platform would be accessible to teaching teams and authorized personnel in order for them to determine the support required to students.

    Examples:

    ○ *The limitations of current regulatory approaches voiced by the research participants indicate the need for a more flexible and responsive …*

    ○ *In view of the concern of the survey respondents, it is clear that …*

    ○ *The counternarratives expressed by participants underscore the importance of …*

    ○ *The findings from the literature review revealed that the existing frameworks for … remain fragmented and reactive.*

- Describe the path forward and evidence each aspect of it with the data you collected. You can further strengthen the path forward with relevant literature. For example:

A two-way digital platform designed to facilitate interaction between dyslexic students and staff offers a transformative approach to inclusive education. The first aspect of the platform is its dialogic nature; this was inspired by six of the participants who lamented the 'top-down one-size-fits-all' approach of disability support. Their remarks about their perceived lack of agency when engaging with disability support has also been noted in the literature (Arthurs, 2025; Huda and Arthurs, 2023). The second aspect …

← The path forward

← Evidenced by your data and relevant literature

- Describe the limits of your path forward.

    Examples:
    - *Due to the homogeneous background of the research participants, the model may not account for …*
    - *Since the respondents were recruited from a specific setting, the model may not be applicable in other …*
    - *While the model provides useful insights, it may not fully represent the broader population because of the small sample size of research participants.*

5.5 Another path

- State any unexpected discoveries of interesting issues that are slightly outside your objectives or research questions. For example, you may be focused on a specific process, then surprisingly you notice a reoccurring topic in your interview transcripts. However, if you investigate this topic, it will take you away from your research objectives. So, this is the section to provide a brief overview of this discovery.

    Examples:
    - *The most surprising aspect of the students' responses was their consistent mentioning of the lack of professional development of their lecturers that inhibited their progress.*
    - *While my dissertation was primarily focused on team collaboration processes, I unexpectedly discovered the influence of underlying social dynamics.*
    - *Although the primary focus of the dissertation was on the effectiveness of remote working practices, I observed emerging mental health concerns among participants.*

    Examples:
    - *What is surprising is that …*
    - *One unanticipated outcome was that …*
    - *What is curious about this result is that …*
    - *This result was unexpected and suggests that …*
    - *One unexpected outcome was the extent to which …*
    - *Contrary to expectations, this study found that …*

- State why your discovery is significant to the field.

    Examples:

    - *The discovery of self-care practices amongst healthcare workers is significant because it broadens our understanding of the resilience and resourcefulness of workers in stressful work environments.*
    - *This discovery is crucial as it uncovers hidden challenges that can impede the effectiveness of the complaints process.*
    - *This discovery is important because it can improve the practical application of the research findings.*
    - *This discovery is significant because it contributes to an interdisciplinary understanding, showing how different fields interact with the core topic.*

- State the need for further research of your discovery.

    Examples:

    - *This revelation warrants further investigation with a larger …*
    - *This discovery is a potentially fruitful avenue for future research in …*
    - *This is an important issue for future research …*
    - *Future research questions should include …*
    - *Several questions remain unanswered at present …*
    - *Further work should be undertaken to investigate the …*
    - *A further study with more focus on … is therefore suggested.*

5.6 Conclusion

- Summarize this chapter.

    Examples:

    - *The following conclusions can be drawn from this research …*
    - *This research has identified …*
    - *This research has shown that …*
    - *The research indicates that …*
    - *The findings of this research suggest that …*
    - *Overall, this research strengthens the idea that …*
    - *The findings of this research support the idea that …*
    - *This research has raised important questions about the nature of …*

- Explain the usefulness of your research.

    Examples:
    - *The findings will be of interest to …*
    - *The insights gained from this study may be of assistance to …*
    - *The findings of this research provide insights for …*
    - *These findings have significant implications for the understanding of …*
    - *This research sheds new light on …*
    - *The understanding gained should help to …*
    - *The research contributes to the understanding of …*
    - *These results contribute to the expanding field of …*
    - *This research is among the first comprehensive investigation of …*
    - *This research is among the first detailed accounts of …*
    - *By providing a model of practice, this research offers a novel understanding of …*

- Escort the reader to the conclusion chapter.

    Examples:
    - *Moving on to the final chapter, the overall contributions of this dissertation will be summarized and reflected on.*
    - *The following chapter will consolidate the insights of this research, offering a final assessment of the contributions and outlining recommendations for further investigation.*
    - *The concluding chapter will provide a holistic summary, evaluating the study's overall impact and exploring the next steps for advancing knowledge in this area.*

Template 2: The Findings/Results chapter and Discussion/Analysis chapter are merged into one chapter

This template is for those that want to combine the Findings/Results and Discussion/Analysis into one chapter. This chapter will be titled the Findings/Discussion chapter or Results/Analysis chapter, etc. You will present your findings in a paragraph(s), then in the following paragraph(s), you will analyse your findings. Therefore, you are talking about a similar topic/theme in two ways; descriptively in the first paragraphs and analytically in the following paragraphs. Describe, then analyse, describe then analyse, and so on. For example:

> **4.1 The impact of remote working on employee well-being**
>
> > **Paragraph 1:** <u>Describe</u> your survey responses on the impact of remote working on employee well-being.
>
> > **Paragraph 2:** <u>Analyse</u> your survey responses on the impact of remote working on employee well-being.
>
> **4.2 Organizational support to enhance employee well-being while remote working**
>
> > **Paragraph 3:** <u>Describe</u> your survey responses on organizational support to enhance employee well-being while remote working.
>
> > **Paragraph 4:** <u>Analyse</u> your survey responses on organizational support to enhance employee well-being while remote working.

The Findings/Discussion chapter
4.0 Introduction

- State the aim of this chapter.

  Example:
  - *This chapter presents and analyses the key findings of the research on postgraduate international students.*

- Explain how this chapter is arranged.

  Example:
  - *The findings are organized around the research objectives outlined in the introduction chapter. Each section will address each objective, presenting the data collected, then offering insights into the data. The chapter commences with a discussion on the frequency of the consumer use of fitness apps. The second section investigates the relationship between digital fitness and traditional forms of fitness (in-gym) in the aftermath of the pandemic. Finally, the chapter examines the factors driving the fitness apps following the pandemic, while identifying potential implications for both theory and practice.*

4.1 The heading of this section is derived from your research objective or research question

For example, if your research question is: *What is the role of ethics in the development of cloud-based typing assistants?* then your heading could be: *4.1 The role of ethics in the development of cloud-based typing assistant.* Alternatively, if your research objective is: *To identify the challenges of cultural awareness in coaching*, then your heading could be: *4.1 The challenges of cultural awareness in coaching.*

- This section *describes* the findings from your surveys, interviews, questionnaires, focus groups, etc. To accentuate your description of the data, you can use quotes, paraphrases, narration, graphs, tables, charts, etc. Make sure that the findings in this section align with the heading of this section.

    Examples:
    - *The results of this survey show that …*
    - *The first part of the questionnaire revealed that …*
    - *This survey did not detect any evidence of …*
    - *There were some negative comments about …*
    - *The participants on the whole demonstrated …*
    - *Only a small number of respondents indicated that …*
    - *Most participants agreed with the statement that …*

- This section *analyses* the above findings. Select one of the approaches detailed on pages 187–192 to analyse your findings (analysing statements, conflict, agreement, prevalence, wider context or conceptualization).

    Examples:
    - *These conflicting findings could be associated with the nature of the …*
    - *A possible explanation for this might be that …*
    - *This result may be explained by the fact that …*
    - *Several factors could explain this occurrence. First, …*
    - *These differences can be explained in part by …*
    - *This inconsistency may be due to …*
    - *The reason for this is not clear but it may have something to do with …*
    - *Unfortunately, these findings are rather difficult to interpret because …*

4.2 The heading of this section is derived from your research objective or research question

For example, if your research question is: *What is the role of ethics in the development of cloud-based typing assistants?* then your heading could be: *4.2 The role of ethics in the development of cloud-based typing assistant.* Alternatively, if your research objective is: *To identify the challenges of cultural awareness in coaching*, then your heading could be: *4.2 The challenges of cultural awareness in coaching.*

- This section *describes* the findings from your surveys, interviews, questionnaires, focus groups, etc. To accentuate your description of the data, you can use quotes, paraphrases, narration, graphs, tables, charts, etc. Make sure that the findings in this section align with the heading of this section.

    Examples:
    - *The results of this survey show that …*
    - *The first part of the questionnaire revealed that …*
    - *This survey did not detect any evidence of …*
    - *There were some negative comments about …*
    - *The participants on the whole demonstrated …*
    - *Only a small number of respondents indicated that …*
    - *Most participants agreed with the statement that …*

- This section *analyses* the above findings. Select one of the approaches detailed on pages 187–192 to analyse your findings (analysing statements, conflict, agreement, prevalence, wider context or conceptualization).

    Examples:
    - *These conflicting findings could be associated with the nature of the …*
    - *A possible explanation for this might be that …*
    - *This result may be explained by the fact that …*
    - *Several factors could explain this occurrence. First, …*
    - *These differences can be explained in part by …*
    - *This inconsistency may be due to …*
    - *The reason for this is not clear but it may have something to do with …*
    - *Unfortunately, these findings are rather difficult to interpret because …*

4.3 The heading of this section is derived from your research objective or research question

For example, if your research question is: *What is the role of ethics in the development of cloud-based typing assistants?* then your heading could be: *4.3 The role of ethics in the development of cloud-based typing assistant*. Alternatively, if your research objective is: *To identify the challenges of cultural awareness in coaching*, then your heading could be: *4.3 The challenges of cultural awareness in coaching*.

- This section *describes* the findings from your surveys, interviews, questionnaires, focus groups, etc. To accentuate your description of the data, you can use quotes, paraphrases, narration, graphs, tables, charts, etc. Make sure that the findings in this section align with the heading of this section.

    Examples:
    - *The results of this survey show that …*
    - *The first part of the questionnaire revealed that …*
    - *This survey did not detect any evidence of …*
    - *There were some negative comments about …*
    - *The participants on the whole demonstrated …*
    - *Only a small number of respondents indicated that …*
    - *Most participants agreed with the statement that …*

- This section *analyses* the above findings. Select one of the approaches detailed on pages 185–190 to analyse your findings (analysing statements, conflict, agreement, prevalence, wider context or conceptualization).

    Examples:
    - *These conflicting findings could be associated with the nature of the …*
    - *A possible explanation for this might be that …*
    - *This result may be explained by the fact that …*
    - *Several factors could explain this occurrence. First, …*
    - *These differences can be explained in part by …*
    - *This inconsistency may be due to …*
    - *The reason for this is not clear but it may have something to do with …*
    - *Unfortunately, these findings are rather difficult to interpret because …*

4.4 The path forward

This section seeks to offer a solution, model, articulate a new vision, convey a new direction, or reimagine an issue. You are at a unique vantage point; you have read the relevant literature, collected data and analysed it. This places you in the best position to make an informed offering; this section symbolizes your unique contribution to existing knowledge. This section may involve describing a framework of engagement, model of practice, model of institution, model of behaviour, mode of praxis, code of practice, etc. You do not have create a path forward completely from scratch; you can repurpose or adapt something that is already in existence.

- Articulate the rationale for a path forward. You will need to make explicit that the data you collected indicated a need for an intervention or rethinking. For example, the neurodivergent students that you interviewed spoke about their frustrations of having to disclose their diagnoses to lecturers for reasonable adjustments to made. This would happen every time they changed modules. Therefore, as a path forward, you describe a two-way secure digital platform where students can upload their diagnosis, necessary accommodations and comments. This platform would be accessible to teaching teams and authorized personnel in order for them to determine the support required to students.

    Examples:

    - *The limitations of current regulatory approaches voiced by the research participants indicates the need for a more flexible and responsive …*
    - *In light of the concern of the survey respondents, it is clear that …*
    - *The counternarratives expressed by participants underscores the importance of …*
    - *The findings from the literature review revealed that the existing frameworks for … remain fragmented and reactive.*

- Then describe the path forward and evidence each aspect of it with the data you collected. You can further strengthen the path forward with relevant literature. For example:

> A two-way digital platform designed to facilitate interaction between dyslexic students and staff offers a transformative approach to inclusive education. The first aspect of the platform is its dialogic nature; this was inspired by six of the participants who lamented the 'top-down one-size-fits-all' approach of disability support. Their remarks about their perceived lack of agency when engaging with disability support has also been noted in the literature (Arthurs, 2025; Huda and Arthurs, 2023). The second aspect ...

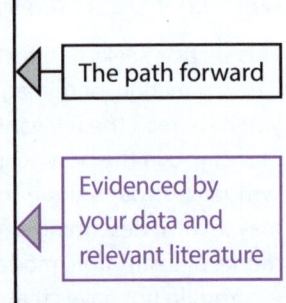

- Describe the limits of your path forward.

    Examples:

    - *Due to the homogeneous background of the research participants, the model may not account for ...*
    - *Since the respondents were recruited from a specific setting, the model may not be applicable in other ...*
    - *While the model provides useful insights, it may not fully represent the broader population because of the small sample size of research participants.*

4.5 Another path

- State any unexpected discoveries of interesting issues that are slightly outside your objectives or research questions. For example, you may be focused on a specific process, then surprisingly, you notice a reoccurring topic in your interview transcripts that falls slightly outside your aim. So, this is the section to provide a brief overview of this discovery.

    Examples:

    - *The most surprising aspect of the students' responses was their consistent mentioning of the lack of professional development of their lecturers that inhibited their progress.*
    - *While my dissertation was primarily focused on team collaboration processes, I unexpectedly discovered the influence of underlying social dynamics.*
    - *Although the primary focus of the dissertation was on the effectiveness of remote working practices, I observed emerging mental health concerns among participants.*

Examples:
- What is surprising is that …
- One unanticipated outcome was that …
- What is curious about this result is that …
- This result was unexpected and suggests that …
- One unexpected outcome was the extent to which …
- Contrary to expectations, this study found that …

• State why your discovery is significant to the field.

Examples:
- The discovery of self-care practices amongst healthcare workers is significant because it broadens our understanding of the resilience and resourcefulness of workers in stressful work environments.
- This discovery is crucial as it uncovers hidden challenges that can impede the effectiveness of the complaints process.
- This discovery is important because it can improve the practical application of the research findings.
- This discovery is significant because it contributes to an interdisciplinary understanding, showing how different fields interact with the core topic.

• State the need for further research of your discovery.

Examples:
- This revelation warrants further investigation with a larger …
- This discovery is a potentially fruitful avenue for future research in …
- This is an important issue for future research …
- Future research questions should include …
- Several questions remain unanswered at present …
- Further work should be undertaken to investigate the …
- A further study with more focus on … is therefore suggested.

4.6 Conclusion

• Summarize this chapter.

Examples:
- The following conclusions can be drawn from this research …
- This research has identified …
- This research has shown that …
- The research indicates that …

- The findings of this research suggest that …
- Overall, this research strengthens the idea that …
- The findings of this research support the idea that …
- This research has raised important questions about the nature of …

- Explain the usefulness of your research.

  Examples:
  - The findings will be of interest to …
  - The insights gained from this study may be of assistance to …
  - The findings of this research provide insights for …
  - These findings have significant implications for the understanding of …
  - This research shed new light on …
  - The understanding gained should help to …
  - The research contributes to the understanding of …
  - These results contribute to the expanding field of …
  - This research is among the first comprehensive investigation of …
  - This research is among the first detailed accounts of …
  - By providing a model of practice, this research offers a novel understanding of …

- Escort the reader to the conclusion chapter.

  Examples:
  - Moving on to the final chapter, the overall contributions of this dissertation will be summarized and reflected on.
  - The following chapter will consolidate the insights of this research, offering a final assessment of the contributions and outlining recommendations for further investigation.
  - The concluding chapter will provide a holistic summary, evaluating the study's overall impact and exploring the next steps for advancing knowledge in this area.

47 How to write the conclusion chapter

The conclusion chapter is a summary and synthesis of the entire dissertation. This chapter should not contain information that has not been discussed in earlier chapters.

Conclusion chapter template

5.0 Summary of findings

- Summarize your central findings.

Example:

This study has qualitatively examined children's views on obesity. Results found that children have well-developed perceptions of the identity, cause, timeline, consequences and control/cure of obesity but which nevertheless differ from adult understandings of obesity.

Examples:

- ○ *This dissertation set out to …*
- ○ *This dissertation has argued that …*
- ○ *This dissertation has discussed the reasons for …*
- ○ *The aim of the dissertation was to examine …*
- ○ *This project was undertaken to design …*

5.1 Contribution to the field

This section is about the unique contribution that your dissertation will make to the field or subject area. This is an opportunity to blow your trumpet.

- State what is unique about your dissertation.

    Examples:

    - ○ *Unlike previous studies on large language models, this dissertation focuses on the biases of academic English.*
    - ○ *The originality of this dissertation lies in its methodological innovation, employing a postcolonial approach to understand the experiences of junior academics.*

- *By focusing on the gender dynamics in business strategy, my dissertation challenges conventional management theories and introduces a revised paradigm for understanding organizational success.*
  - *This dissertation offers a novel perspective by integrating the fields of neurodiversity and race in higher education.*
- State who will benefit the most from your dissertation. Are there governmental and non-governmental entities, policymakers, professionals or professional bodies that will benefit from your research? Can your study improve or account for practice in a particular industry?

Examples:
  - *Public health officials can use the findings from this dissertation to design more effective interventions targeting mental health in Roma communities.*
  - *This dissertation will be of great benefit to curriculum developers, offering new methods to integrate technology into curriculum design for enhanced student engagement.*
  - *Tech startups looking to scale up and bring their products to the market will benefit from the survey data from venture capitalists.*

5.2 Broader implications of research

Beyond your field or subject area, what is the broader lessons that we can learn from your findings? What is it about your findings that would be of interest to wider society? In the above sections, you summarized the findings that were specific to your research and talked about your contribution to the field, but in this section, you should take a wider view. For example, few people would care about your contribution to management theory or that 200 of your respondents commented on their remote work arrangements, but wider society would be interested in the broader changing landscape of the workplace. One broad implication is sufficient. Do not make the broad implication too outlandish or too detached from what you have discussed because you should not include new or unconventional information to your conclusion.

Here are some examples of possible broad implications:

- Your broad implication can be identifying the 'real' issue; the 'real' issue that you point to is a root cause or foundational issue that gives rise to other issues.
- Your broad implication can be that the future looks bleak; your research has led you to conclude that the future looks bleak because there is no indication of reform or there is a failure to undertake the type of radical

action needed. There is no planned legislation or government enquiry; there is nothing on the horizon.

- Alternatively, your broad implication may be that your research has led you to believe that the future looks promising; perhaps you have observed the setting up of government committees, planned legislation, increased awareness, etc.

- Another implication is that an issue has been underestimated. Your research has revealed that the real extent of this issue is largely unknown or maybe the focus is on one particular aspect, whereas you have identified a more problematic aspect that has not been widely discussed.

- Alternatively, your research revealed that the problem or issue has been overstated or amplified; there are more troubling matters that we need to focus on.

- Another implication is that the focus should be on the system or the environment, not the individual. Your research revealed that even though individuals have been labelled or stigmatized, the real issue is systemic.

- Another implication is that the issue a growing ethical dilemma. Your research reveals a crossroads; in order to progress, an ethical choice has to be made. As a society, we must choose a path.

5.3 Limitations

State the limitations of your dissertation. The limitations are the boundaries, constraints and potential shortcomings of your research. Just one or two limitations are fine. Do not overstate or exaggerate limitations – this will significantly devalue your dissertation.

Common limitations:

- Methodological limitation: Constraints related to research design, data collection or data analysis methods that may have negatively impacted your findings.

- Sampling limitations: Constraints related to sample sizes that impact the generalisability of findings or sampling approaches that may lead to some bias.

- Time limitations: Limited time available to conduct the research that negatively impacted the data collection or depth of analysis.

- Access limitations: Difficulty in obtaining specific data or resources, access to participants that restrict the scope of the research.

Example limitation sentences:
- The dissertation did not engage with …
- This study was not able to encompass the entire …
- Several problems arose when collecting the …
- Establishing … is beyond the scope of this dissertation.
- The small size of the responses meant that it was not possible to …
- It is beyond the scope of this research to examine the …
- The reader should bear in mind that the dissertation was focused on …
- A potential problem is that the scope of this dissertation may be too broad.
- Due to resource constraints, this dissertation did not provide a comprehensive review of …

• State the future research needed to address the above limitation(s).

Examples:
- This is an important topic for future research …
- Research questions should include …
- Further research is required to establish the …
- Further research should be undertaken to investigate the …
- Therefore, it is suggested that further research is needed with more focus on …
- Further studies on this topic are therefore recommended.

5.4 Recommendations

This section is for you if your dissertation addressed a problem or something to be improved. We put forward recommendations to address problems or improve upon something.

Two to four recommendations are sufficient. Recommendations should be tied to the problems or situations that you have mentioned throughout your dissertation. In other words, every recommendation should be linked to something that you have explicitly discussed in previous chapters. Every recommendation should be conservative, practical and achievable. Additionally, you do not have to create recommendations from scratch; you can point to an actual example documented in the academic literature, government reports, NGO reports, PhD studies, etc. Be sure to reference the source of your borrowed recommendations.

- State two to four recommendations. A recommendation consists of two aspects: (1) what is needed to fix the problem, (2) a brief explanation of the logic that led you to the recommendation.

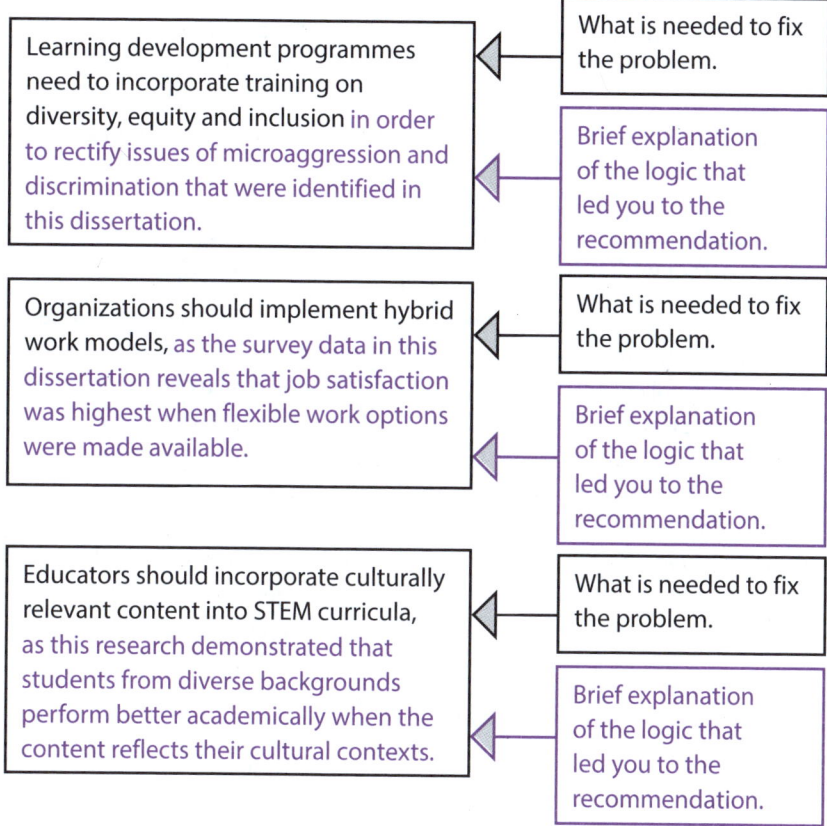

48 How to write an abstract

The abstract is a summary of the entire dissertation. It provides an overview of the main elements of the dissertation, allowing readers to quickly grasp the main points and significance of the work. Typically, the abstract is around 150–300 words, written in past tense and comes before the introduction chapter. It can either be written as one normal paragraph or a paragraph with headings, for example:

Abstract with headings

Purpose: The article qualitatively examined the ways in which primary school children perceive obesity. **Design/methodology/approach:** The study was qualitative in nature; semi-structured interviews were conducted with 33 children.

Findings: It was found that experience contributed to the detailed knowledge of overweight children's perceptions of cures of obesity.

Practical implications: Future childhood obesity interventions can utilize these findings to create campaigns and strategies that are more consistent with children's understandings of this condition.

Originality/value: To the author's knowledge, no previous study has examined children's perceptions of obesity beyond perceived causes.

Abstract without headings

The article qualitatively examined the ways in which primary school children perceive obesity. The study was qualitative in nature; semi-structured interviews were conducted with 33 children. It was found that experience contributed to the detailed knowledge of overweight children's perceptions of cures of obesity. Future childhood obesity interventions can utilize these findings to create campaigns and strategies that are more consistent with children's understandings of this condition. To the author's knowledge, no previous study has examined children's perceptions of obesity beyond perceived causes.

An abstract consists of six sections:

1. Provide a brief background to the topic of your dissertation. This sentence or two gently introduces the reader to the topic. For example, if your dissertation evaluates the impact of technological advancements on patient care in the UK, you can provide a brief background to the topic: *Technological advancements have revolutionized patient care in the United Kingdom, transforming the way healthcare is delivered and experienced …*

2. State the central aim of the dissertation in a concise sentence.

    Examples:
    - *The aim of this dissertation was to …*
    - *This dissertation set out to examine …*
    - *This research set out to determine whether …*
    - *The principal objective of this research was to investigate …*
    - *The study aimed to explore the relationship between …*

3. State the methodology/methods you used to collect data.

    Examples:
    - *Data for this study were collected using …*
    - *This dissertation employed survey methodology to investigate the impact of …*
    - *This research takes the form of a case study …*
    - *The dissertation is based on four case studies.*
    - *This investigation used a phenomenological approach to identify the …*
    - *An online survey provided responses from 350 participants.*
    - *A combined qualitative and quantitative methodological approach was used to …*
    - *The data in this dissertation was drawn from four main sources …*
    - *This research uses interviews to produce an account of …*

4. Provide an overview of your central findings.

    Examples:
    - *The findings showed that …*
    - *This research identified …*
    - *Respondents reported that …*

- The dissertation concludes that …
- The findings presented here confirm that …
- The findings identified limited evidence of the …
- The principal findings of this research are that …

5. State the uniqueness of your research.

   Examples:
   - The findings can contribute to a better understanding of …
   - This dissertation provides a timely and necessary study of the …
   - The findings presented in this study add to our understanding of …
   - The research findings represent a further step towards developing …

6. State who would find this research useful. Are there governmental and non-governmental entities, policymakers, professionals or professional bodies that will benefit from your research? Can your study improve or account for practice in a particular industry?

   Examples:
   - Public health officials can use the findings from this dissertation to design more effective interventions targeting mental health in Roma communities.
   - This dissertation will be of great benefit to curriculum developers, offering new methods to integrate technology into curriculum design for enhanced student engagement.
   - Tech startups looking to scale up and bring their products to the market will benefit from the survey data.

Conclusion

We have explored a range of hacks and approaches to enhance your academic writing without having to rely on AI. While AI may seem like a tempting shortcut, the techniques in this book empower you to write with originality, efficiency and sustainability. Mastering these skills not only improves your academic success but also prepares you for real-world communication beyond university. Keep practising, stay resourceful and trust in your own ability to produce great work.

Index

analysis
   analysis section in dissertation 179–204
   critical analysis of texts 75–88
argumentation 55–73
assignment 33–53
   types of assignments 35–6
   understanding your assignment task 37–41
   command verbs 38–9
   structure of assignments 42–53
   introduction 42–7
   main body 48–50
   conclusion 51–3

book reviews 24–5

concept 89–102
critical analysis 75–88
   criticizing models, theories, frameworks and concepts 101-2
citation 5
   in-text citation 5
   location of in-text citation 5
   common mistakes in citation 5
command verbs 38–9
context 11–12

discussion 179–204
dissertation 131–212
   abstract 210–12
   introduction 140–9
   literature review 150–62
   methodology 163–78
   results 179–204
   conclusion 205–9

evidence 1–4
   definition of evidence 1
   types of evidence 3–4
   context of evidence 11–12

findings 179–204
frameworks 89–102

google books 17–23
government sources 28–9

journal articles
   journal article hack 31–2
   using journal articles as evidence 3

models 102

paraphrasing– 9
PhD thesis 26–7

quoting 9
   avoidance of quoting 9

'real world'
   real world information 30
   real world argument 68–9

reference 5
   full reference 5
reflection 105–30
   reflective models 105–8
   zooming out to the wider literature 109–11
   choosing between two paths 112–13
   articulating doubt 114–16
   creating themes 117–19
   bad practice vs best practice 120–21
   incorporating statements 122–5
   incorporating different perspectives 124–27
   uncovering power 128–30
reporting verb 7–8
research 15–32
   abstract 210–12
   research aim 133–9
results 179–204

search terms 15–16

theories 89–102